AN INTRODUCTION TO
THE HISTORICAL
BOOKS OF THE
OLD TESTAMENT

AN INTRODUCTION TO
THE HISTORICAL
BOOKS OF THE
OLD TESTAMENT

ROBERT L. CATE

BROADMAN
&HOLMAN
PUBLISHERS

Nashville, Tennessee

© Copyright 1994
BROADMAN & HOLMAN PUBLISHERS
All rights reserved

4210-44
0-8054-1044-9

Dewey Decimal Classification: 222
Subject Heading: BIBLE. O.T. HISTORICAL BOOKS // HISTORY
Library of Congress Catalog Number: 93-44233
Printed in the United States of America

Library of Congress Cataloging-in-Publication Data
Cate, Robert L.
    An introduction to the historical books of the Old Testament / by Robert L. Cate.
        p.   cm.
    Includes bibliographical references and index.
    ISBN 0-8054-1044-9
    1. Bible. O.T. Historical Books—Introductions.   I. Title.
BS1205.2.C37   1994
222'.061—dc20   93-44233
                                                        CIP

To
Ray Young

whose appreciation of the past
and whose hope for the future
make my present ministry possible

Contents

Preface

People do not write books just for the fun of it. Writing is hard work. While it may be a labor of love, it is a labor nonetheless. Furthermore, except for fiction, people seldom read books just for the fun of it. Readers are trying to fulfill an assignment, to learn something, or to answer questions. To accomplish any of these purposes, reading also becomes hard work. Therefore, since both writing and reading are hard work, you may legitimately ask why I wrote this book and why you should read it. These are reasonable questions, and you should expect a thoughtful answer to them. Further, you deserve these answers before you invest your time and energy in the study of this book.

Need.—For most Christians, the Old Testament is a closed book. Since we are New Testament Christians, we often reason, why should we bother with studying the Old Testament at all? However, for most of us this is usually a futile attempt at self-justification. In our more honest moments, we are well aware that the Old Testament is the root from which the New Testament grew. To understand the New Testament fully, most of us are really aware that we must be familiar with the Old.

For most Christians, though, the Old Testament still remains an essentially closed book. It covers so many centuries and deals with so many foreign people who had customs radically different from ours that we generally find it beyond our comprehension. Admittedly, some of us may find meaning in the great narratives of Genesis 1—11. Others certainly find excitement and even significant truths in the adventures of Abraham, Isaac, Jacob, Joseph, and Moses. The Ten Commandments frequently stir us with a sense of what life should and could be like. Occasionally, the preaching of an Amos, an Isaiah, a Jeremiah, or an Ezekiel will prick our consciences. We may even rejoice at the praises of the psalmists and find guidance in the practical wisdom of the book of Proverbs.

The history books of the Old Testament are a different matter altogether for most of us, however. While the stories of Joshua and Samson, Samuel and David, or Ahab and Josiah may be exciting, we find it next to impossible to relate these to anything relevant to our lives.

Thus this book may well meet your need. The books identified as Old Testament history books are closed books for most of us. They are in our Bibles, but they are not in our hearts and minds. They seldom bring God's Word into our lives. Being in our Bibles at the very least means that they are a step in God's ongoing revelation of His purposes. They are a step in the development of the people who gave birth to Jesus of Nazareth. These facts alone mean that we should study them.

Granting this, however, why can we not get along with the introductions to the Old Testament which have already been written? Certainly, introductions to the entire Old Testament deal with this subject. However, as they deal with all of the Old Testament, such books contain a great deal more material than this one does, This book is focused upon the historical books of the Old Testament specifically. Further, it seeks not only to introduce these books, it also seeks to follow the ongoing story which is found in them. This latter feature is not normally found in the typical Old Testament introduction.

On the other hand, commentaries related to one or more books of this collection do deal with the introductory material related to each book. However, several different commentaries would have to be purchased to get the introductory material related to the entire collection of these books. Further, with their focus upon the minute details of each passage in a book, it becomes very difficult to follow the basic story told in the book. Readers often get bogged down in detail, failing to see the overall themes for the mass of information provided. That is one of the things which frightens people away from this material in the first place.

Of course, any good history of the Old Testament era will follow the basic story line and themes of these books. However, such books will present significantly more detail as regards to archaeology and related history, while leaving out the introductory material dealing with the individual biblical books with which we will deal. In short, no book is available which deals with the Old Testament history books in the manner which is planned here.

Nature and Purpose.—The first purpose of this book is to fill the gap and meet the need described above. This volume is intended as a textbook for college or seminary classes dealing with the Old Testament history books. A second and subsidiary purpose is to provide a source for serious students of the Bible who wish to study this part of the Bible on their own. The third purpose is to provide a review for pastors, Sunday School teachers, and other Bible students who have covered some of this material in the past. I hope to refresh their memories and to add the details of new developments in the field. The scholar in the field may find help here in review but must remember that this is intended first and foremost to be an introduction.

The plan of the book has been designed to achieve the purposes I have described. Each biblical book in the series beginning with Joshua and continuing through Esther will be introduced in the light of the best biblical scholarship. Following this, the story of each will be summarized, bringing in where relevant the present results of archaeological and historical research.

The same basic outline for presenting the information relating to each book will be followed throughout. This will allow the student dealing with the entire collection more easily to master the material. At the same time, it will allow those who are interested in only one book of the collection to deal with it in one place without having to skip throughout the book to various passages.

The student is reminded that this book is not intended to replace the study of the biblical text itself. To the contrary, I have intended to provide an aid to the study of the Bible. You will need to read the biblical text along with this book throughout your study.

Author's Background and Presuppositions.—For you to be better able to evaluate this book and its presentation, you need to know something of me and of the presuppositions I bring to this task. I am a Christian who was trained as an electrical engineer before I responded to God's call into ministry. After graduating from the seminary, I served fifteen and a half years as pastor of two churches, one located in Georgia and the other in South Carolina. Following that, I served as professor of Old Testament at Golden Gate Baptist Theological Seminary for ten years and then was Dean of Academic Affairs for six additional years.

During my last two years at Golden Gate, I became concerned with what was and was not happening for the cause of Christ on the campuses of our major secular universities. As a result, I began to urge Ph.D. students to give serious thought and prayer toward such a ministry for themselves. God once again demonstrated that He has a sense of humor when I was called to fill the chair of religion at Oklahoma State University.

For all of my ministry, I have been convinced that God's primary call to me was and is to make the Bible come to life for people. As a pastor, professor, administrator, and writer, that has been my goal and purpose. It is my fundamental purpose as I undertake the writing of this book. I approach the book believing that God is, that He loves you and me, and that He has revealed His perfect will through the Bible. I also believe that both you and I are sinners and that God has redeemed us through His Son, Jesus, who is both the Lord of the universe and of the church. I believe that, having accepted Jesus as my Lord, I have an obligation to share the good news of His salvation with those who neither accept nor know Him. Finally, for our purposes in this book, I believe that God will reveal Himself through His Word to those who seek Him with all their hearts.

From this foundation, then, I invite you to join me in the study of these fascinating but neglected books in God's Word. The history books of the Old Testament are a part of that Word. We can never hear Him speak through them until we first begin to read and study them.

Chapter 1

Introductory Matters

History is not a subject that interests, much less excites, most people. We are frustrated by strange names, confused by innumerable dates, and bored by dry-as-dust tales of events long gone. This is especially true when these events appear to have little or no meaning for us or the world in which we live.

Those of us who turn to the Bible as God's Word to humanity may be more motivated to read biblical history because we are seeking to hear God's voice as He reveals His will to us. Even that commitment, however, leaves most of us hurrying through the Old Testament history books in an attempt to find something that more nearly touches our hearts, such as the uplifting phrases of the Psalms, the stinging words of the prophets, or the reflective bits of wisdom found in Proverbs. The sad truth is that by proceeding with such haste and disinterest, we not only miss some exciting stories, we also miss receiving a significant portion of God's revelation to us.

How Is History Written?

Most people, at first glance, think that they know what history is and that scholars agree on how it should be written and studied. A few seconds of thought, however, may help them see that these assumptions are wrong. Those who write history, write it for a purpose. Therefore each author picks and chooses events that help tell the story. Different purposes of the writers will make the stories read differently simply by the materials that they choose to record. It makes all the difference in the world to read the history of the Civil War written by one sympathetic with state's rights as contrasted with a similar record written by one who upholds the unity of our country. Further, although it ought not to be so, some historians are not above bending facts or even "inventing" them to prove their point. The various approaches to the story of the Nazi Holocaust of World War II give abundant evidence of this

Therefore, those of us who study history not only need to become familiar with the facts of that history, we also need to try to understand the message that the author or editor is communicating. Furthermore, when this approach is applied to the history books of the Bible, we must also add our desperate need to hear the message of the Divine Author. If these books are God's Word, then we have the task of listening to that word with as much understanding as is possible..

Glossary	
History Books	Joshua, Judges, Ruth, Samuel, Kings, Chronicles, Ezra, Nehemiah, Esther.
Masoretic Text	The edition of the Hebrew Bible copied about A.D. 1000 and used as the basis of modern scholarly study.
Canon	A collection of authoritative books believed to preserve God's teachings for our lives. Christians call the Old and New Testament their canon.
Pentateuch	First five books in Hebrew Bible (Genesis, Exodus, Leviticus, Numbers, Deuteronomy), also known as Torah or teaching.
Former Prophets and Latter Prophets	Two subsections of the Prophets, the second major part of the Hebrew Bible.
Former Prophets	Joshua, Judges, Samuel, Kings.

Glossary	
Latter Prophets	Isaiah, Jeremiah, Ezekiel, and the Book of the Twelve (Hosea, Joel, Amos, Obadiah, Jonah, Micah, Nahum, Habakkuk, Zephaniah, Haggai, Zechariah, and Malachi).
Writings	Third and final major part of the Hebrew Bible includes Psalms, Job, Proverbs, the Five Megilloth read at annual Festivals (Ruth, Song of Songs, Ecclesiastes, Lamentations, Esther), Daniel, Ezra, Nehemiah, Chronicles.
Deuteronomic History (DH)	Modern scholarly name for the Old Testament books of Joshua, Judges, Samuel, and Kings. The name is based on the similarity in language and theological emphases between these books and Deuteronomy.
Deuteronomic Historians (DTR)	Persons who put Deuteronomic History in its final shape.
Cultus or Cult	The worship practices of a specific people in a specific worship place.
Septuagint	Earliest Greek translation of the Old Testament, possibly done in Alexandria, Egypt, about 200 B.C.
Vulgate	Latin translation of the Bible based on the work of Jerome about A.D. 400 and used by the early Roman Catholic Church as the official text of Scripture.
Criticism	The serious study of a subject by a person with intense interest in the subject or the method used in intense study.

Scope and Nature of Old Testament History Writing

The Books to Be Covered

The history books of the Old Testament that form our present concern are found in our English Bibles between Deuteronomy and Job. These twelve books are Joshua, Judges, Ruth, 1 and 2 Samuel, 1 and 2 Kings, 1 and 2 Chronicles, Ezra, Nehemiah, and Esther.

We might assume that these books should tell an ongoing story starting in Joshua and continuing uninterrupted through Esther. As we read through these books, however, we find some surprises. Ruth did not live at the end of the period of the Judges but fits somewhere back in its middle. First Chronicles does not pick up where 2 Kings leaves off. In fact, the narrative of 1 Chronicles actually goes back to Adam. Its contents overlap all of the preceding history books, and its main narrative parallels 2 Samuel through 2 Kings. A difference exists, however. After the kingdoms of Israel and Judah divided, the Books of Chronicles followed the history of Judah only, referring to the Kingdom of Israel where they came into contact with their southern sister.

Distinctions Among the History Books

When we begin to examine the history books more thoroughly, we discover that in the traditional Masoretic text (MT) of the Hebrew canon, they are not collected in the same place. They follow one another in English Bibles because early English translators followed the order of the Septuagint, the earliest Greek translation of the Old Testament. Frequently the English translators found this order as they worked in the Vulgate, the Latin translation used as the official text of the Roman Catholic Church at that time. The Hebrew placement of these books may reveal what the ancient Hebrews thought of these books and what they understood God was revealing through them.

In the Hebrew canon Joshua, Judges, 1 and 2 Samuel, and 1 and 2 Kings follow Deuteronomy, forming the second section of the Hebrew Bible. Ancient Hebrews named this section, "The Former Prophets." Books in the other portion of this second section are called "The Latter Prophets" and include Isaiah, Jeremiah, Ezekiel, and The Twelve (Minor Prophets). The ancient Hebrews believed that all of these books had something in common: their prophetic theme. In the history books the Hebrews heard a message that reminded them of the message(s) in the books describing the ministries and preserving the messages of those whom we consider to be the great prophets.[1]

The location in the canon of these six books should make us ask the important question: was their primary purpose to record history, or was it to proclaim God's revelation found in that history? Old Testament scholars have discovered another significant feature about these books that may also be indicated by their location in the MT. Following immediately after Deuteronomy, these six books show a consistent tendency to apply the values, judgments, and commands of Deuteronomy in assessing the strengths and weaknesses and the successes and failures of those who sought to lead God's people. Because of this, many Old Testament scholars refer to these books as the Deuteronomic History (DH). Further, the authors and editors of these books are often referred to as the Deuteronomic Historians (Dtr).

The other six history books (Ruth, Ezra, Nehemiah, 1 and 2 Chronicles, Esther) appear in the Hebrew Bible in the third section known as "The Writings." This points to something different about these six books. Further, the books of Ruth and Esther are found in a subcollection of The Writings called "The Megilloth" or "the Five Scrolls." These differing canonical locations alert us that ancient Israel saw something different in these books. As we read the books, we sense significant differences in the way they are written and in what their apparent purposes were. Ruth and Esther are magnificent stories, each with one heroine and each focusing on a very narrow portion of ancient Israel's story. On the other hand, 1 and 2 Chronicles, Ezra, and Nehemiah deal with the broader sweep of history.

While the narrative of 1 and 2 Chronicles overlaps the books of the Deuteronomic history, they tell it from a wholly different perspective. Joshua, Judges, 1 and 2 Samuel and 1 and 2 Kings have a prophetic outlook on Israel's history while 1 and 2 Chronicles, Ezra, and Nehemiah tell Israel's story from the standpoint of the Levitical priesthood. Their concerns call attention to the ritual and worship of Israel, particularly as seen by the citizens of Jerusalem. (This combination of ritual and worship is called "cultus" or

---

1. William Sandford LaSor, David Allen Hubbard, and Frederic William Bush in *Old Testament Survey* (Eerdmans Publishing Company, 1982) have a good but brief discussion of what the classification of "Former Prophets" appears to communicate, 190–93.

"cult" by Old Testament scholars. We will use that term from here on.)   Putting the prophetic and priestly perspectives in parallel gives us a fuller picture of that history, just as putting the four gospels together gives us a fuller portrait of the life and ministry of Jesus.

The Nature and Purpose(s) of Old Testament History

What were the authors and editors of the Old Testament history books trying to accomplish with these books? Asked in another way, why do we have the twelve Old Testament history books in our canon?

We can approach this question from the perspective of faith. The Old Testament is a part of the Bible, God's revelation. If these twelve books are only seeking to inform us of the events in Israel's history, then we really don't need them. Many of the events reported here are recorded in other ancient records. Thus the theologian would tell us that we have these books because God had something to reveal to us. Israel's history books are one of the vehicles by which He makes that revelation.

We can also seek for an answer to our question in the pages of the Bible itself. John, in the fourth gospel, tells us quite precisely what his purpose in writing was:

> Now Jesus did many other signs in the presence of his disciples, which are not written in this book. But these are written so that you may come to believe that Jesus is the Messiah, the Son of God, and that through believing you may have life in his name. (John 20:30–31)

With these words, John asserted that his purpose was to point his readers to Jesus. Furthermore, he did this in an attempt to lead them to have life through their faith in Jesus. Finally, he bluntly asserted that he chose some events and omitted others to achieve his purposes.

Can we transfer John's purpose to the Old Testament writers?   The Gospel of John is a part of the same Bible as Joshua. Luke wrote about Jesus Himself, walking with two disciples on the way to Emmaus: "Then beginning with Moses and all the prophets [which at the very least included Joshua through 2 Kings], he interpreted to them the things about himself in all the scriptures" (Luke 24:27). Thus, according to Jesus Himself, the Old Testament pointed to Jesus.

Pointing to Jesus may be the precise focus of Old Testament history. Consider, for example, two kings of the Northern Kingdom of Israel, Omri and his son Ahab. The books of Kings deal with Omri in seven verses (1 Kings 17:22–28). His son Ahab, on the other hand, has parts of seven chapters devoted to him (1 Kings 16:69—22:40). An immediate appraisal might conclude that Ahab was far more important than his father Omri. Assyrian records present a different perspective. For more than a century afterwards they referred to Israel as "the land of Omri." This leads some to ask, "Is the Bible wrong?" Or, "Were the Assyrians wrong?"

The answer is that neither was wrong. Assyria was writing history from a human perspective. The Bible emphasized what God was doing with and through His people. Ahab was not important for who he was or what he accomplished. He happened to reign while God was working through Elijah and Elisha. What we call Old Testament history was written to tell us what God was doing in human history and what His acts mean to us now.

Both biblically and theologically we conclude that the Old Testament history books are in the Bible primarily as revelation, helping people see God and understand His work and His will. We study and read this material first and foremost to hear God speak to us. Throughout our study, our prayer must be that of the boy Samuel, "Speak, for your servant is listening" (1 Sam. 3:10). We are not merely trying to find out what happened; we are trying to find out what God did in those events and what He is saying to us through them.

Features of Old Testament History Writing

Acknowledging this as the purpose of Old Testament history, we also need to consider its nature. Several features stand out about Old Testament history and Old Testament historiography. (Historiography is the science of writing history.)

First, Old Testament history writers were selective in their choice of details. They reported what was of importance to the message they were communicating. For example, Exodus 2:1 reports the marriage of Moses' parents, followed by his birth in the very next verse. After reading these verses one might think that Moses was their first child. We later discover, however, that he had an older sister and an older brother (Ex. 2:4; 6:20; 7:7). The births of these two other children were unimportant to the author's message in chapter 2. This omission of unnecessary details appears to be true throughout all the Old Testament history books. Thus we must be alert for such occasions.

A second closely-related characteristic of Old Testament historiography is that of compression. Writers frequently omitted large blocks of time from their narratives because the historical data from that period did not add to the message they were communicating. Again, the author of Exodus reports Moses' flight from Egypt this way: "But Moses fled from Pharaoh. He settled in the land of Midian, and sat down by a well" (Ex. 2:15). Nothing is told about the danger and difficulties of the hundreds of miles of desert through which he traveled on foot to get to that well in Midian. The hard journey may have been important to Moses while it occurred, but it was outside the purpose for writing Exodus. The same thing is noted in the story of Moses' marriage (Ex. 2:20–22). Moses had dinner with the priest of Midian, married his daughter, and fathered a son, all in three verses.

A third feature of Old Testament history writing is the problem of contemporaneous events. Events going on in two separate places at the same time have to be written down one after the other. They simply cannot take up the same space on the same page. This is quite obvious as we consider the parallel reigns of the kings of Israel and Judah. This may not be so obvious as we deal with other events and times. There is always a possibility that two events told one after the other may have occurred at the same time but in different places.

A fourth feature of Old Testament historiography is the author's focus. Events that seem to be unimportant from the standpoint of a secular historian are very important to the biblical author's report. In the report of the battle of Jericho, it would appear to be of little significance that a man named Achan stole some of the possessions of the people of Jericho (Josh. 7:1). This moral and cultic lapse, however, was of major significance in Israel's relation to God. Thus the Bible devotes several verses to it. We must constantly remind ourselves that the author is communicating a message.

These features of Old Testament history must be kept in mind if we are not going to be led astray in our study. We must not become confused by the fact that Old Testament history is revelation more than record. If we do not keep this concept before us, we shall have difficulty understanding the message(s) of the books we are about to study.

The Study of Old Testament History Books

In studying these twelve books, the Old Testament scholar must consider several different disciplines. These are normally called *criticisms*. Unfortunately, criticism has negative connotations in the minds of many people. To avoid this, let us remember that to be a *critic* is not to be opposed to something. To be a critic is to be so intensely interested in something that you study it seriously. Old Testament criticism refers only to the serious study of the Old Testament by persons intensely interested in the nature and meaning of the Old Testament.[2]

The first two disciplines used to study these books are textual criticism and linguistic criticism. *Textual criticism* is the study of ancient manuscripts to determine as nearly as possible what words the original manuscript contained. *Linguistic criticism* takes the original text determined by textual criticism and studies its grammar, syntax, word meanings, idioms, and the like to determine as precisely as possible what the original author or editor meant.

Having determined what a text says and what it means, the Old Testament scholar brings another series of disciplines into play. *Literary criticism* studies the text from the standpoint of literary categories such as prose and poetry. It deals with such issues as whether we are dealing with songs or narrative (Josh. 10:12b–13a,16–21). Finally, it deals with issues such as the sources from which a book was drawn, its date of writing, and who wrote it. These kinds of information any student of literature, biblical or otherwise, must know to understand the text's purpose and meaning.

Closely related to this is *historical criticism*. (Some Bible students join literary and historical efforts together as *literary-historical criticism*.) Historical criticism seeks to understand the message of the biblical text through the study of other ancient records and of the results of archaeology. A major purpose of such study is the discovery as nearly as possible of exactly what did happen. For example, Paul wrote to the Romans, "Christ died for the ungodly"

2. A thorough approach to Old Testament criticism from an evangelical position can be found in Amerding's *The Old Testament and Criticism* (Eerdmans Publishing Company, 1983).

(Rom. 5:6). The historical critic looks at this theological statement and notes that the event was that Christ died. All other records, including the gospels, are brought to bear to discover how and when Christ died. Roman records could show the nature, meaning, and normal emotional reaction to crucifixion.

Beginning with the work of Hermann Gunkel in 1906, *form criticism* came to be used in an attempt to discover the common forms used in the oral transmission of biblical material before it was written. Such study discovered that material with common subjects came to be passed on in similar literary forms. Developing from this, *redactional criticism* began to analyze the differences between the use of forms as they reveal the purpose and human nature of the authors and editors who handled the material. *Rhetorical criticism* analyzes the principles and rules of speech and writing as well as literary devices authors use to give life, nuances, and meaning to texts. Repetition, analogies, alliteration, and literary structures create emotional reactions for the reader and guide the reader to understand the points the writer wishes to emphasize.

At least three new disciplines have been added to these earlier ways of studying the Old Testament. The first of these is *canonical criticism*. *Canonical criticism* recognizes that each passage and book in the Old Testament is ultimately a part of an entire authoritative collection of books. A book or a section of a book must ultimately be studied not as an isolated part but in its relation to the entire collection. How does its message fit into the whole? How does reading the Pentateuch prepare one to read the history books? How does knowing the New Testament story affect your reading and interpretation of the Old Testament history books?

Related to this is *reader response criticism*. This seeks to approach a text not from the perspective of its author but from the perspective of its readers. These were the people who heard the voice of God speak through text and treasured it. Why did the ancient readers preserve the book at all? How did the book change their beliefs and actions? How did it affect their relationships to God and to other people? The same questions can be asked concerning the responses of modern readers.

A third new area of critical study is called *structuralism*. Structuralism is an attempt to study the deep, hidden, or unconscious structure of a passage in an attempt to get into the subconscious depths of a passage or text. Those who seek to use it have not even been able to agree on a definition of what they are about. Until clarity in approach and results can be achieved, we do not consider its use appropriate for an introduction like this volume.

In the material that follows all of these approaches to the study of the text, with the exception of structuralism, will be used. In most instances, however, involving the reader in their use is the task of a commentary, not that of an introduction. Rather than go into the details of such study over and over again, we shall refer to these various ways of studying the text only where they are of extreme importance.

The Importance of Old Testament History

Throughout the study we will use various methods to show the context, the dates, the people, and the events of Israel's history. As we write and as you read, we must constantly remind ourselves that history is important in the Old Testament (and in the New) because God revealed Himself in mighty acts. The Bible is not a book of theology. The Bible is God's self-revelation through His relations with His people and their response to Him. For Israel, God was met before He was thought about. That is true for us as well. Thus we must study these books to see what He did and what He is saying to us through those events. Should we learn the events and miss their meaning for us, we will fail the course in Old Testament history books.[3]

Questions for Review and Reflection

1. Why can two quite different histories be written by good historians about the same events?

2. Name the history books in the Old Testament. Do they follow one another in the Hebrew text of the Old Testament? Why?

3. What methods do scholars use to study the history books and other Old Testament literature? What is the purpose of each method? Why are the methods called criticisms?

---

3. A helpful addition for understanding the background and context of the Old Testament history books is a good knowledge of the geography of the religion. One of the better sources available is Dennis Baly's, *Geography of the Bible* (Harper & Brothers, 1957).

4. Why do you want to study the historical books? What do you expect to learn from them? Do they really serve as a canon for your life?

Chapter 2

The Book of Joshua

All that most people know about Joshua is some rather fuzzy details about the battle of Jericho, based more on an old Afro-American spiritual than on the Bible. That is sad, for the book reports on one of the more important eras in Hebrew history. This book tells how the "chosen people" received the "promised land". Throughout the rest of Israel's history, the only thing more important to them than the fact that they were the people of God was that the land was God's gift to them. In fact, that belief still lies behind much of the present crisis between modern Israel and her Arab neighbors. That alone should send students of the Bible to study its pages.

From a religious perspective, the most important feature of the book may not be the story of the conquest. The Pentateuch (the first five books of the Bible) directed our attention ultimately to God's covenant commitment to His people and their corresponding covenant commitment to Him. The Book of Joshua calls our attention not only to the conquest of the land but to the great ceremonies of covenant renewal in which Joshua led his people. All of the events of the conquest led to this great "Event." God's covenant did not end with the death of Moses. Neither did it end with Israel's entry into Canaan. The point for Israel (and for us) is that God had the same commitment with them and expected the same commitment from them even when their circumstances changed, when they ceased being wanderers and became a settled society

Glossary	
Covenant	The promises and commitments God made with His people. The most important covenant agreement was made on Mount Sinai (Ex. 19—34) establishing the identity and limits of God's people as people of Yahweh, the God of Israel.
Conquest	The series of events through which the landless people of God gained control of Palestine under Joshua's human leadership and God's miraculous divine leadership.
Transjordan	Land east of the Jordan River.
Cisjordan	Land west of the Jordan River.
Tribe	Sociological designation of a political organization of a kinship group for social, political, and religious life. Israel's twelve tribes each traced origins to one son of Jacob as related in Genesis 25—50.
Yahweh	Personal name of Israel's God, often printed as LORD with small caps.
Wilderness Wandering	Israel's forty years of existence in the desert area south of Palestine caused by their repeated refusal to believe and obey God (see Num.13—14).
Manna	Special food God provided for the people of Israel to eat in the wilderness (see Ex. 16).
Cherem	Transliteration of Hebrew word describing war practice in which all spoils of war were destroyed, symbolizing their being devoted to God rather than to human materialism and greed. Some of Israel's neighbors had a similar practice.

Glossary	
Historiography	The science of writing history. When applied to a specific author or editor, it refers to the method or approach used by that person in writing history.

Place in the Canon, Date, and Authorship

The book receives its name from the central figure of the book, Joshua. In both the Hebrew and the English canon, Joshua follows immediately after Deuteronomy. This location is intensely significant insofar as the Hebrew canon is concerned, for this location makes it the first book of the second major section of the Hebrew canon, known as The Prophets. Joshua is also the first book of the sub-section called The Former Prophets. Its place in the canon should alert us that the ancient Hebrews saw it as more than a mere recitation of historical events. They saw a proclamation from God, a proclamation in some way understood as being similar to the Book of Isaiah, the first book of The Latter Prophets. We must not forget this as we study the book.

An unbroken tradition extending from the biblical era to the Age of the Enlightenment ascribes the authorship of the book to its central figure, Joshua. Thoughtful study of the book, however, reveals that the Bible does not identify who wrote Joshua. Two references, sometimes cited as throwing light on the issue, are actually of little benefit. Joshua is said to have written "a copy of the law of Moses" (8:32). This was written on stones, not on a scroll, and can in no way refer to the book itself. Others point to the statement that "Joshua wrote these words" (24:26). What he wrote were the "statutes and ordinances" of the covenant. These were written in a book of the law of God (24:25–26). Furthermore, the death and burial of Joshua is recorded (24:29–30). Obviously, Joshua did not write this about himself.

Since the rise of literary criticism, some scholars have sought for a continuation in Joshua of the so-called strands or sources that they claim appear in the Pentateuch. This effort, however, has led to no consensus, proving essentially fruitless.

What can be determined by a careful study of the biblical text is that knowledge of many of the events came from Joshua in some instances and in other instances from Joshua or from people who were involved in those events. Much of the historical and geo-graphical detail appears to come from eyewitnesses. On the other hand, frequent references to things that are still in existence or are done "to this day" appear to indicate that a final editing, if not the final writing, was done long after the events occurred. (Compare 4:9; 5:9; 6:25; 7:26; 8:28–29; 9:27; 10:27; 13:13; 15:63; 16:10.) The book cites at least one source, the Book of Jashar, from which a quotation was taken (10:13; compare 2 Sam. 1:17–27; 1 Kings 8:12–13). The Book of Jashar appears to have been an anthology of poems dealing with great events in Israel's past. It had to have been completed long after the event referred to in Joshua.

As we have noted, Joshua, along with the other five books of The Former Prophets, has a decidedly Deuteronomic flavor, generally evaluating Israel and their leaders in terms of Deuteronomy. Although we have no way of knowing precisely when and by whom the book was written, it appears that it was completed sometime during the monarchy by Israel's Deuteronomic historians. Anything more precise than this is pure guesswork.

Organization of the Book

Joshua continues the story of the Hebrew people following the death of Moses. Beginning with the call to leadership of Joshua, it tells the story of Israel's entry into western Canaan, her essential conquest of the land, and the division and assignment of the land among the tribes. These events appear to be centered around and lead up to the two great ceremonies of covenant renewal, where Israel reaffirmed their commitment to Yahweh their God (8:30–35; 24:1–28). Some interpreters suggest that these are two reports of the same event, but they do not appear to be.

The structure of the book may be seen in the following outline. We will use this outline as the basis of our study of the contents of the book.

    I. Israel's entry into western Palestine (1:1—8:29)

        A. Joshua's commissioning (1:1–9)

        B. Organizing the people (1:10–18)

        C. Spying out the land (2:1–24)

        D. Entering Canaan (3:1—5:12)

        E. Conquest of central Canaan (5:13—8:29)

    II. The covenant ceremony at Shechem (8:30–35)

Summary of Contents

The Book of Joshua continues the story of the Hebrew people following the death of Moses. Shortly before his death, Moses had assigned part of the Transjordan region to the tribes of Reuben, Gad, and half of Manasseh. Following that he addressed all Israel on the plains of Moab, challenging them to be faithful to God's covenant with them (Num. 32:1–42; Deut. 1:1; 6:1–15; 34:1–8).

I. Israel's Entry into Western Palestine (1:1—8:29)

The book begins with Yahweh's commissioning of Joshua to begin the task for which he had been called: leading Israel in the conquest of Canaan (1:1–9). Joshua's name means "Yahweh saves" or "May Yahweh save." The Hebrew word was transliterated centuries later into Greek and then more centuries later into English as Jesus. Prior to Moses' death, Joshua served as a military captain under Moses. After Moses' death the task of leadership was his. Apparently it terrified him. This may be reflected by the fact that three times in this call experience God admonished him to be strong and courageous (1:6,7,9). The basis for his faith and confidence was to be the law of God.

Immediately after God's commissioning, Joshua organized his people as an army for the task before them (1:10–18). He also reminded the people of Reuben, Gad, and the half-tribe of Manasseh that they had promised to accompany their fellows in the task of conquest, being assured that they would be faithful to those commitments. They, too, seemed to have sensed Joshua's sense of fear at the task before him. As a consequence, they also urged him to be strong and courageous as he faced the task God had given him. Both God and Israel assured Joshua that real courage does not lie in being unafraid. To the contrary, it lies in being faithful even when you are fearful.

As a good military commander, or as a good leader in any circumstance, Joshua sent trusted followers to find out all they could before making the initial attack on Canaan at Jericho (2:1–24). The spies sent into the land found shelter from a prostitute named Rahab. She saved the Hebrew spies from the Canaanites, who would have killed them, demonstrating that even society's outcasts can do good things. Recognizing that these men were servants of God, she asked for their help in protecting her and her family in the conflict to follow. Granting her request, the spies fled, first going into the hills above Jericho for three days until the pursuit ended.

Following the report from his spies, Joshua led the people of Israel across the Jordan (3:1—5:12). From the outset, he repeatedly reminded his people that what was about to happen in Canaan was God's wondrous act, not their achievement (3:5). The first demonstration of God's power was in the miraculous crossing of the Jordan. Even in the midst of Israel's advance, Joshua paused to set up a memorial commemorating God's miraculous power. The memorial stone would help parents educate their children and would bear testimony to "all the peoples of the earth" of God's mighty power (4:21–24).

Joshua also paused to circumcise the men of Israel (5:2). Apparently, those who had wandered in the wilderness had not participated in this rite that sealed their covenant with God. It was imperative that those who were a part of God's people be willing to be identified with God's people. The people of Israel also observed the Passover to remember and celebrate God's deliverance from slavery in Egypt (see Ex. 12—15). Both of these ritual acts reaffirmed their covenant commitment.

At this time the wilderness wandering officially ended, for God's provision of manna stopped (see Ex. 16). At long last, Israel was in the land to which Yahweh had been leading them all along. They no longer needed His special provision. Past miracles are important for faith, but they become unnecessary when God has fulfilled His promises in present situations.

Preparations complete, Joshua finally led Israel in the attack on central Canaan (5:13—8:29). This began with the miraculous victory at Jericho (6:8–21). One of the strangest features of this victory was that God wanted Israel to destroy everything in the city. Faithful Rahab and her family were the only exceptions (6:17–19). This total destruction was also a concern of Deuteronomy (Deut. 20:16–18), one more indication of the relationship between the two books. This belief that God would destroy so wantonly sounds utterly foreign to us. It rested on the ancient Hebrew concept of *cherem*, a "devoted" or "sanctified" thing. This means that anything that God designated as *cherem* belonged wholly to Him. The people of Israel were not allowed to enrich themselves with either property or slaves from any place designated as *cherem*. While clearly not of New Testament standards, such practices were common in the ancient Near East and must be judged against that background and that time. It was intended to keep Israel pure from idolatrous and pagan contamination.[1]

Joshua's army proceeded into the central highlands with an abortive attack on Ai/Bethel (7:2–26). Compared to the attack on Jericho, this should have been an easy victory. Israel's defeat, therefore, utterly dismayed the people. After investigation, they discovered that sin had caused their defeat. Achan had violated the *cherem* (7:1,10–12,24–25).

The sin of one man made all Israel guilty. This sense of corporate responsibility runs deep throughout the Old Testament. The people of Israel purged their sin by punishing Achan. Not only was Achan executed, his family and all that he possessed were destroyed. By violating the *cherem* he had become *cherem*. Sin is never to be taken lightly.

Joshua next led Israel in a renewed attack on Ai/Bethel. This time they were victorious (8:1–29). Some difficulty exists from an

---

1. While Von Rad popularized the concept of "Holy War" in the Old Testament, a good summary of the present understanding of the concept can be found in Kaiser's *Toward an Old Testament Theology* (Zondervan Publishing House, 1978), 134–36.

archaeological perspective as to which city Joshua actually attacked. Many archaeologists do not believe Ai was occupied during Joshua's time. Excavation results may indicate that Bethel rather than Ai was attacked. Since Ai means "ruin" and since these two cities were located on adjacent hilltops, almost never being inhabited at the same time, the names may have been used interchangeably at this time of history. With this victory Joshua and his armies were firmly lodged in central Canaan.

II. The Covenant Ceremony at Shechem (8:30–35)

Following the initial battles, Joshua and the people of Israel marched twenty-five miles northward through what should have been enemy territory to Shechem. There they held a great ceremony of covenant renewal with half of the people on the slopes of Mt. Ebal and the other half on the slopes of Mt. Gerizim. Shechem, a major Canaanite city-state, was located in the valley between these two mountains. All this marching and worshiping was apparently done quite peacefully. How was this possible?

Archaeological evidence and the study of other biblical passages have convinced some Old Testament scholars that not all of Israel remained in Egypt for the entire four hundred years. They believe that Shechem (and some other places) was already inhabited by Hebrews who had come into the land much earlier. If this is so, the purpose of the great covenant ceremony was not only to reaffirm the commitment of the Hebrew people led by Joshua—it may also have been intended to include those who had not originally been a part of the covenant, having come into the land earlier. In any case, Joshua and his army paused to give thanks and to reaffirm their commitment to the God who was giving them their land.

III. Concluding the Conquest of Palestine (9:1—12:24)

Israel's victories had essentially divided northern Canaan from southern Canaan. They now controlled the main highway down the mountainous backbone of the land. Their victories had at least gotten the attention of some Canaanite city-states and struck terror into the hearts of others. The people of Gibeon through deceit and trickery got Israel to enter into a covenant of peace with them (9:1–27). Israel's failure was that they had become over-confident in their own abilities and wisdom and "did not ask direction from the Lord" (9:14).

When the people of Israel discovered what had happened with the Gibeonites, they still kept their word, showing a deep reverence for honor and integrity. On the other hand, because of the treachery of these new neighbors, Israel did not allow them the full status of equality in the land.

Because of the treachery of the Gibeonites, other Canaanite kings sought to destroy them (10:1–27). Joshua immediately sought to fulfill his oath to the Gibeonites and came to their defense. Once again God's intervention gave Israel victory.

At this point, Joshua and his people set out to conclude the conquest of southern Canaan (10:28–43). The line of cities he attacked—Makkedah, Libnah, Lachish, Eglon, Hebron, and Debir—all sat at the entrance of a valley or on a highway leading from the coastal plain into the central hill country of the south. With these victories, Joshua had successfully isolated southern Canaan from any outside help. Excavations in this region, while not uniform in evidence, give a general picture of an overthrow of many cities shortly after 1250 B.C. When these cities were overthrown, the new culture that took their place was not as advanced as the one that had been defeated. We would have expected precisely this situation if a group of freed slaves had destroyed cities that had been inhabited for a long period of time by a settled and advanced culture.[2]

Following the southern campaign, Joshua then moved his army to the northern border of the land, attacking and defeating Hazor (11:1–15). Hazor was the major fortress on the northern highway leading into Canaan. One of the largest cities in the entire region, it was inhabited by about forty thousand people and was strongly fortified. That victory was one of Joshua's greatest. He again showed his military ability in that he did not attack this city until his troops had gained a significant amount of military experience.

With the defeat of Hazor, all the major border fortresses of Canaan had been defeated. This totally isolated the land from any

2. A more thorough discussion of Joshua's conquest from the standpoint of the archaeological evidence can be found in "The Cities Joshua Conquered," by Cate, in *The Biblical Illustrator* (Summer 1981); Diana Vikander Edelman, ed. "Toward a Concensus on the Emergence of Israel in Canaan," *Scandinavian Journal of the Old Testament* 2 (1991), 1-116; Israel Finkelstein, *The Archaeology of the Israelite Settlement* (Jerusalem: Israel Exploration Society, 1988); Bruce K. Waltke, "The Date of the Conquest," Westminster *Theological Journal* 52 (1990), 181-200.

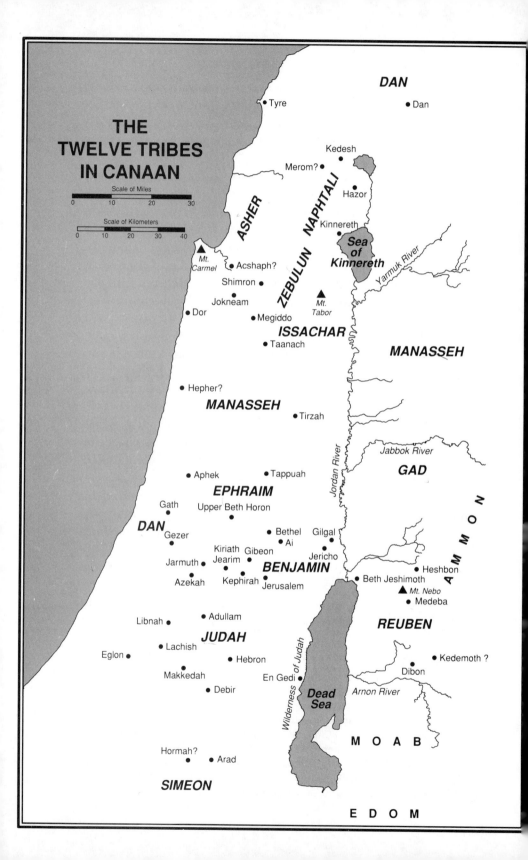

outside help. We are now confronted with a problem as to the ultimate nature of the conquest. The text sums it up by saying that "Joshua took all that land" (11:16). Shortly thereafter, we are told that "very much of the land still remains to be possessed" (13:1). Which report is correct? Some have suggested that we have two different traditions of the conquest that are in conflict. From a military perspective, both reports were true. The land had been essentially taken by isolating it from outside relief. On the other hand, a great deal of "mopping up" needed to be done before Israel actually possessed every village and town.

This part of the book ends with a list of all the kings whom Joshua had defeated. This would have been amazing at any time. For a group of freed slaves wandering in from the desert to accomplish this makes it even more amazing. Looking at their victories forces us to acknowledge that God had given them amazing aid.

IV. Dividing the Land (13:1—22:34)

We have no way of knowing the time that elapsed between 12:34 and 13:1. Joshua was approaching the end of his life. God commissioned him to prepare Israel to move on in their pilgrimage of faith without his leadership (13:1–7). One mark of a great leader is the ability to prepare followers to carry on after him. For Joshua, this meant assigning the various portions of the land to the tribes, clans, and families of Israel.

The text reminds us that half of Manasseh, Gad, and Reuben had already received their portions in the Transjordan region from Moses (13:8–33). Joshua assigned western Palestine to the remaining tribes (14:1—19:51).   The details of these assignments are generally of little significance except to students who wish to major on geographical or archaeological studies of Palestine. Three features of significance catch our attention as we survey this material.

- First, for the first half of this century, some scholars have suggested that Israel did not control enough of this land in Joshua's time for him to have made these allotments. They date these lists to the exilic era and see them as an idealized picture of the time of Joshua. More recent and thorough geographical and archaeological studies, however, reveal that all of the places listed were under Israelite control during the time of David's kingship. There is no reason not to see them as actual assignments made in the time of Joshua. While not often under total Israelite control, they were at least under sufficient control to see them as being assigned for "mopping up."

- Second, Caleb's request is quite fascinating (14:6–15). He and Joshua were the two spies Moses sent into Canaan who believed they could take the land (Num. 13:30; 14:24). Caleb was obviously an old man, since he had survived the wilderness wanderings. Based on his faithfulness and age, he could have requested an easy possession. To the contrary, however, he asked for the most difficult part of the land for himself and his family. Not ready for the retirement he had earned, he sought for a position requiring courage and responsibility to the end of his life.

- Third, Yahweh provided places in the assignment of the land for the study of His Law and for the particular practice of mercy. Under the ancient law codes, a person guilty of killing someone else was to have been killed by the next-of-kin, often called "the avenger of blood." Cities of refuge, however, gave a place of protection for those who had killed "without intent or by mistake" (20:3). God was already working out ways of maintaining justice while practicing mercy and forgiveness. Further, the Levites were the tribe responsible for serving as priests to the rest of Israel. Forty-eight cities were provided for them throughout all the rest of the tribal allotments. These cities were probably intended not only to afford income and sustenance for the Levites, but to serve as centers of worship and to study God's Law. In a real sense, the Levites in their cities were to be the spiritual leaven of Israel.

V. Commitment and Covenant Renewal (23:1—24:33)

Nearing the end of his life, Joshua faced the unfinished mopping-up operations by assigning specific regions of the land to each tribe. Apparently, Joshua did not die as early as he had expected. Watching the tribes go about their combined tasks of settlement and the final defeat of the Canaanites, he realized that their faith was growing cold, so he called for a major assembly at Shechem (23:1—24:33). This time his purpose was not administrative but spiritual.

Some scholars have sought to identify this assembly with that recorded earlier in the book (8:30–35). This is unlikely since both the context and the content of the two events, with the exception of the covenant renewal, are different. Significantly, both of these assemblies were held at Shechem. This may support the contention that here was an older Israelite center.

Joshua began by reminding the people that their victories in the conquest had been wholly due to God's power, not to their own skill or ability. Based on God's mighty acts, he admonished his people to be faithful to Yahweh and to love Him (23:3–13). Love is not merely a New Testament concept. Joshua also warned his people of the ultimate consequences of faithfulness and of disloyalty (23:14–16). This concept of blessing and curse was drawn directly from the pages of Deuteronomy (Deut. 28:1–68).

Following his message, Joshua called on his people for a response, a specific recommitment to their covenant with Yahweh. Joshua set the example by pledging his own commitment, saying, "As for me and my household, we will serve the Lord" (24:15). In this confrontation with Israel, Joshua showed himself not only to be a good leader but to be a master of oratorical skills.

The book then draws to a close with the report of Joshua's death and burial, along with the final details that had to be taken care of before the whole episode of the exodus and the conquest could be brought to a conclusion (24:29–33). God is not merely the God of mighty acts, He is also the God of detail as well.

Message

Two things often stand in the way of those who seek to hear God's message from Joshua. The first of these is the continuing failure of most believers to understand that Old Testament history books are in the Bible as a part of God's revelation. The second is that the nature of the conquest seems so different from the New Testament concept of love toward one's enemies. To this latter objection we can only respond, "Of course it is!" If the message of the New Testament were totally in the Old, we would not have needed the New at all. The conquest must first be understood in the terms of its times.

The first objection is simply an attitude that we must overcome by effort and experience. Only as we hear God speak in books such as Joshua will we overcome our reluctance to listen.

The following are the major parts of God's message I hear in Joshua. Your reading and study should reveal other themes.

1. The basic and underlying theme of the book appears to be that God can be depended on. He keeps His promises.

2. God uses those whom He has chosen, allowing them to be a part of His ongoing kingdom's work.

3. God bestows His gracious gifts on those who will accept the gifts through obedient action.

4. God chooses for His people leaders who are appropriate to the need of the moment and the opportunity that is there.

5. God expects and demands that His people maintain their covenant commitment to Him in both bad times and good times.

6. God blesses or punishes His people based on their response to Him.

7. God's leaders leave the scene with time, but God's work goes on.

Joshua as an Individual

Not all that we know of Joshua is found in this book. He was Moses' military commander in the time of the exodus (Ex. 17:9). In this book, however, we see characteristics of Joshua that made him a good servant of God. As such, he became a good leader, functioning well in the place to which God had called him.

Although frightened at the prospect of leading Israel following the death of Moses, Joshua accepted the call of God to become His servant at that critical time. His years of serving with Moses prepared him to accept new responsibilities. His faith in God seems to have been quite strong. We must note, however, that after the initial defeat at Ai, he utterly failed to understand what had happened. Even then he did not turn against God but took his questions to God. Joshua showed that he had prepared his skills as a military leader for such a time. A former slave in Egypt, he had learned generalship both through experience and through thought. He was ready when the opportunity came. This is revealed by the fact that he planned his campaigns carefully and gathered the best information possible. Even today, were it not for airplanes, the best strategy for taking the land of Israel would be to cut it off from the outside world by controlling all the highways into the main part of the land.

Joshua also proved himself to be an able administrator. When he was unable to lead his people further, he organized them to carry on the task that they had been given. A good leader is always willing and ready to share his responsibility, to prepare his people to function without him, and to step out of their way when the time is right.

Further, Joshua remembered his past. Remembering what God had done gave him hope for and faith in the future, in what God would do. He had learned through his own experience that God is faithful; therefore, he could call on his people to trust God.

Finally, Joshua showed that he was not merely a military leader but a spiritual one as well. He meditated on God's Word (1:7–8). He called on his people for total commitment, setting the example himself (23–24). He did not ask them to do anything that he would not do himself. Given the name "Yahweh saves," Joshua showed by both word and example that this was his confident faith. The hope of the parents who named him became the reality of his life.

Questions for Review and Reflection

1. List the twelve tribes of Israel. Which lived east of the Jordan River? Which lived south of Jerusalem?

2. Trace Joshua's campaign routes on a map of Palestine. What kinds of military strategy did he use to capture the country?

3. What function does the Book of Joshua play as part of the Bible?

4, What does Joshua's understanding of *cherem* and the punishment of Achan say to you about the nature of God? What does it say about the nature of the Old Testament? Compare this to your understanding of God's actions in the final judgment.

Bibliography

Boling, Robert G. *Joshua: A New Translation with Notes and Commentary*. Vol. 6 of *Anchor* Bible, Garden City: Doubleday, 1982.

Butler, Trent C. *Joshua.* in *Word Biblical Commentary*, vol. 7. Waco: Word Books, 1983.

Gray, John. *Joshua, Judges, Ruth.* in New Century Bible Commentary. Grand Rapids: William B. Eerdmans, 1986.

Hamlin, E. John. *Inheriting the Land: A Commentary on the Book of Joshua.* (International Theological Commentary) Grand Rapids: William B. Eerdmans. 1983.

Kent, Dan G. *Joshua, Judges, Ruth.* in *Layman's Bible Book Commentary.* Nashville,: Broadman Press, 1980.)

Soggin, J. Alberto. *Joshua.* in Old Testament Library. Philadelphia: Westminster Press, 1972.

Chapter 3

The Book of Judges

The Book of Joshua records how the "chosen people" *entered* into the "promised land." The Book of Judges describes how they actually *settled down* in it.

The Book of Judges, like Joshua, is relatively unfamiliar to most Christians. They know a little about Samson and his infamous haircut, or at least its more sordid details. They know less about Gideon. The rest of the book with its reports of the folly, sin, and rebellion during Israel's final settlement in Canaan is little more than a series of blank pages in the Bibles of most Christians.

The major focus of the book directs our attention beyond the events of Israel's history to the faith pilgrimage described by that history. Judges centers on Israel's sense of independence from God rather than on their dependence on Him. This basic self-centeredness seems to have characterized the people of God. Victory over their enemies in the major battles of the conquest led them to assume that this was due to their own abilities and prowess rather than to God's presence with them. They believed that they knew what was best for them and how to attain it.

This central theme is clearly set in the final verse of Judges. "In those days there was no king in Israel; *all the people did what was right in their own eyes*" (Judg. 21:25; author's italics). This sense of arrogant independence was founded on a lack of leadership that echoes in a refrain found earlier in the book, "There was no king in Israel" (Judg. 18:1; 19:1). Chaotic times and selfish hearts produced an era of political, social, and religious anarchy. The people of Israel became aimless in their spiritual pilgrimage rather than following the God who had led them from Egypt to Canaan. Judges presents no idealistic interlude in Israel's pilgrimage with God but a realistic time of rebellion.

Glossary	
Cyclic View	Understanding that history has ever-repeating patterns. Baalism taught a cycle of religious rites and nature's processes. Israel's God taught a cycle of human moral decisions and divine actions.
Judge	A person God raised up to bring military deliverance and leadership in time of crisis and oppression.
Baal	Canaanite god whose name meant "husband" or "lord." Each area apparently had its own Baal, who was worshiped in sexual rites expected to bring fertility.
Fertility cult	Worship designed and believed able to ensure that crops, animals, and people reproduced themselves. Often sexual acts were a featured part of worship, seen as symbolic representation of what the god was doing in nature.
Philistines	Part of the Sea Peoples from the northern Mediterranean area. They settled the west coast of Palestine with the Philistines centering in Gaza, Ashkelon, Ekron, Gath, and Ashdod.[1]

1. The Philistines offered a major problem to the people of Israel for an extended period. A thorough study of them may be found by R. A. Kitchen's "The Philistines" in *Peoples of Old Testament Times* (Clarendon Press, 1973), 55–78; T. Dothan and M. Dothan, *People of the Sea: The Search for the Philistines* (New York: Macmillan, 1992); T. Dothan, *The Philistine and Their Material Culture* (New Haven: Yale University Press), 1982; D. Howard, "The Philistines," *Peoples of the Old Testament World,* ed. A. Hoerth, G. Mattingly, and E. Yamauch (Grand Rapids: Baker, 1993).

Glossary	
Midianites	Descendants of Abraham (Gen. 25:2) who settled in the southeastern wilderness below Edom. Moses defeated them (Num. 31:1–8); compare 25:1–18). They used camels to raid Israel, but Gideon drove them back.
Amalekites	Wilderness warriors who constantly opposed Israel (Ex. 17:8–16; Num. 14:39–45; Deut. 25:17–19). Gideon faced these desert raiders.
Amphictyony	Ancient Greek social organization with a loose confederation of tribes centered around a central worship place. Often used as a model to understand Israel's organization in the time of the judges.
Shephelah	Hebrew geographical term meaning "lowland." The low foothills in southwestern Palestine between the Philistine coastal plain and the highlands of Judah to the east.

Place in the Canon, Date, and Authorship

Judges received its name from the function of those persons whom Yahweh raised up to deliver His people from their oppressors. Judges is a part of the Former Prophets in the Hebrew canon along with Joshua, 1 and 2 Samuel, and 1 and 2 Kings. This should alert us that Israel understood the Book of Judges as a part of Yahweh's prophetic proclamation far more than as a mere recitation of historical events. As we study the book, we must seek to hear God's message boldly proclaimed through the events recorded in it.

Early Jewish tradition ascribed the authorship of Judges to Samuel, but the book gives no clue as to the identity of its author. The manner in which it evaluates Israel's sin makes it likely that it is a part of the Deuteronomic history.

The date of the writing of Judges hinges on interpretation of difficult passages and application of scholarly theories. Some of the material is obviously very ancient, apparently from eyewitnesses. Other expressions, however, appear to indicate a time of writing long after the events recorded. The refrain, "In those days there was no king in Israel," seems to reflect an era well after the first appearance of kingship in Israel (Judg. 18:1; 19:1; 21:25). Further, 18:31 seems to indicate that Shiloh was no longer the house of God. That did not occur until at least the time of Samuel (1 Sam 4:12–18).

Some scholars suggest that the statement that the priests of Dan served "until the time the land went into captivity" (Judg. 18:30) indicates that the final writing of the book could not have occurred until the fall of Jerusalem (587/6 B.C.), or at least not until the fall of the Northern Kingdom (722 B.C.). The following verse, however, reveals that this reference was to the fall of Shiloh.

In this century critical scholarship has dated Deuteronomy to the reign of Josiah in 622 B.C. and placed Judges after this. More recent years have seen the scholarly consensus break up into a series of more radical theories. A more appropriate approach would say that the basic core of Deuteronomy must have been present at least in oral form long before 622.

We have no way of knowing precisely when and by whom the Book of Judges was written. It was most likely completed sometime during the monarchy by Israel's Deuteronomic Historians. This could have been as early as the latter days of the united monarchy, but it is more likely to have been done in the era of the divided monarchy. Anything more precise than this is guesswork.

Organization of the Book

Before we deal with the organization and structure of the Book of Judges, we need to consider several related issues. These issues affect our understanding not only of the recorded events but also of the message proclaimed through them.

The main part of Judges (at least chaps. 3—16) has an unusually clear theological structure, letting us see immediately the author's basic message and purpose. Israel's history is presented as a series of recurring cycles. Chapter 2 gives a summary of this cyclic view of history in six distinct steps.

- Sin: "Then the Israelites did what was evil in the sight of the Lord" (2:11). "They abandoned the Lord, and worshiped Baal and the Astartes" (2:13).
- God's wrath: "So the anger of the Lord was kindled against Israel" (2:14).

- Oppressors raised up: "He gave them over to plunderers . . . and . . . into the power of their enemies" (2:14).

- God's mercy aroused: "The Lord would be moved to pity by their groaning because of those who persecuted and oppressed them" (2:18).

- Deliverance: "Then the Lord raised up judges, who delivered them out of the power of those who plundered them" (2:16).

- Sin renewed: "But whenever the judge died, they would relapse and behave worse than their ancestors" (2:19).

The cycle kept repeating itself. Each separate narrative in the book retells this same basic story with different characters acting in different places. Judges' cyclic view of history has been considered by some interpreters to be similar to that of the Canaanites. Anything more than a superficial reading of the book shows that it differs in two major respects. First, Israel's cycle was not automatic. Canaan's was. Canaanite, Baalistic religion saw cycles occurring in the normal processes of nature—growth, death, and renewal of life. Israel's cycle occurred as the result of Israel's deliberate moral choices. Second, Yahweh's responses were not capricious, but were the fulfillment of the promises of His Covenant, particularly as set forth in Deuteronomy. He promised judgment on apostasy and blessing on faithfulness. Even with the repetitive cycles, God was still viewed as being Sovereign, in control of history.

The Nature of a Judge

A judge in ancient Israel was not primarily an official deciding legal issues. Only a very few judges seem to have had this function. The Hebrew text does not use a noun "judge" but uses a verb to describe their function. They "judged" Israel. Their basic function seems to have been that of savior or military deliverer. God used them because they had the "gifts" or talents needed at the moment. Thus Bible students often classify the judges as "charismatic" or gifted leaders. When the basic military crisis was over, they generally faded into the background. They came from varying occupations and stations of life and usually returned when their missions were over.

The judges are usually classified as major or minor judges, depending on the amount of detail given. The major judges are Ehud (3:15–30), Deborah (4:4—5:31), Gideon (6:11—8:35),

Jephthah (11:1—12:7), and Samson (13:2—16:31). The minor judges are Shamgar (3:31), Tola (10:1–2), Jair (10:3–5), Ibzan (12:8–10), Elon (12:11–12), and Abdon (12:13–15). Interpreters disagree as to whether Othniel (3:7–11) is major or minor and whether Abimelech (9:1–57), Gideon's son, is a judge at all. I consider Othniel as a major judge, but do not classify Abimelech as a judge, since God did not raise him up.

Emotional Impact

Another unique feature of Judges is the emotional impact aroused in the thoughtful reader. The inspired author told the stories with details that literally bring us to the stomach-turning point. Graphic descriptions of Ehud's assassination of Eglon (3:15–23), Deborah's joyful song of the brutal murder of Sisera (5:24–27), Jephthah's murder of his daughter (11:30–39), and the numerous gross events in the life of Samson (14:1—16:31), all leave us with a sense of sickening revulsion. Perhaps this emotional response was intended by the author who told the stories in this manner in order to inform us that, if God could use such revolting events and people, He could use revolting, rebellious Israel. If He could use revolting, rebellious Israel, this gives us hope as well.

Chronological Considerations

The chronology of Judges appears to be quite straightforward. Adding up the various periods of the judges' service and the interspersed periods of peace gives a total of 410 years. The Bible also states, however, that Solomon began to build the temple 480 years after the exodus (1 Kings 6:1). Subtracting the supposed time of the judges from this leaves only seventy years to cover Israel's forty years in the wilderness, the time of the conquest, the times of Eli, Samuel, Saul, David, and the first four years of Solomon. This is obviously impossibly short.

A closer reading of the biblical text suggests a solution to our dilemma. Generally only three or fewer tribes were involved in each oppression. In the case of Deborah, where we have the largest number of tribes involved, only ten tribes are listed, and two of these, Machir and Gilead, do not appear in the normal listings of tribes. They may have been clans within a tribe. The point is that most, if not all, of the oppressions seem to have been quite limited in scope. This becomes more probable when we locate the tribes involved in each oppression. The oppressions usually seem to have been regional, with one going on in one part of the country while one or more were going on elsewhere. Obviously, two or more events going on at the same time have to be written about one after the other. Further, given the Old Testament's sense of corporateness, when one part of the nation was attacked, it could be described as all of the nation hurting. When God protected one part of Israel, He protected the nation.

This theory that arose from the biblical material allows the total period of the judges to be significantly less than 410 years. This might be even further reduced. Many numbers in Judges are either forty or some multiple of it (3:11,30; 4:3; 5:31; 8:28; 13:1; 15:20; 16:31). Some numbers in the Bible appear to have a special symbolic or idiomatic meaning. Forty often appears to refer to a long, indefinite period of time or, when coupled with years, may refer to a generation. This would limit the period of the judges to about 200 rather than 410 years. Of course, 40 may also be literal. (A more detailed treatment of the history and problems of the era of the judges may be found in my book, *These Sought a Country: A History of Israel in Old Testament Times* [Nashville: Broadman Press, 1985]).[2]

Canaanite Religion

Throughout their history the Hebrew people were constantly led astray by Canaanite religion, the worship of Baal. Many details of this faith were discovered in a large Canaanite library found at Ras Shamra (the ancient Ugarit). These tablets are dated to about 1350 B.C.

The religion of Canaan featured a fertility cult. People expected their worship to result in the gods bringing fertility to the land, the herds, and the people. The Canaanites worshipped the Baals. From each hilltop a Baal ruled over the surrounding region. These hilltops were the "high places" so often referred to in the Old Testament.

---

2. The most thorough study available of the issues related to the chronology of judges can be found in Malcom Broom's unpublished doctoral dissertation, *The Chronology of the Judges* (Southern Baptist Theological Seminary, 1961). See more recently Eugene H. Merrill, "Paul's use of 'About 450 Years' in Acts 13:20," *Bibliotheca Sacra* 138 (1981), 246-57.

The worship of the Baals was highly sexual, with the priests and priestesses acting as "sacred" prostitutes. The worship involved having sexual intercourse at these high places. Such "worship" had obvious physical attraction. People throughout the ancient Near East commonly believed that various gods were responsible for various areas of human experience. Thus many Hebrews found it quite easy to believe that Yahweh was a God of war and the Baals gods of agriculture and fertility. They apparently turned to the Canaanite Baals for fertility and to Yahweh for defense. God's chosen leaders, however, taught that Baal worship was rebellion against Yahweh. It led Israel away from God and brought judgment on them again and again.[3]

The Oppressors

Israel faced several enemies during this period. Each enemy had its own time of power and its own ways and reasons for oppressing Israel. The Canaanites wanted to regain control of the land, a control Joshua had broken. The Philistines landed on the coastal plain about the same time Israel entered Canaan from the east. They were part of a larger group known from Egyptian sources as the Sea People. Apparently they originally came from Mycenaea with some living in Cyprus or Crete and having at least camped for a time in Lebanon. Scholars have long thought that the Philistines invaded Canaan following an unsuccessful attempt to invade Egypt. New evidence makes it probable that they were sent by the Egyptians as mercenaries to attack the invading Hebrews. They were apparently the first people in the region with the knowledge of iron smelting. This gave them a major advantage in the ancient arms race. (See 1 Sam. 13:19–22.)

Of a quite different nature were the assaults of the Midianites and the Amalekites. They were desert tribes who had no desire to conquer territory. Instead, they looked for plunder and food, especially at harvest time. Finally, the Transjordan nations of Edom,

---

3. A more detailed summary of Canaanite religion is found in Millard's "The Canaanites," in *Peoples of Old Testament Times* (Clarendon Press, 1973), 43–47. More recent works downplay the sexual nature of Canaanite religion: Alan M. Cooper, "Canaanite Religion," *Relgions of Antiquity*, ed. Robert M. Seltzer (New York: McMillan, 1989), 80–95; Mark S. Smith, *The Early History of God* (San Francisco: Harper & Row, 1990); Karen van der Toorn, "Prostitution (Cultic)," *The Anchor Bible Dictionary* 5 (New York: Doubleday, 1992), 510–13; but see John Day, "Canaan, Religion of," *The Anchor Bible Dictionary* 1, 831–37.

Moab, and Ammon seem to have primarily been venting their inherent enmity against Israel. They seem to have attacked when Israel had first been weakened and demoralized by the assaults of others.

The Judges narrative, however, never focuses primarily on the assault of an external enemy. Such assaults provided the historical event for the faith proclamation that God was using these oppressors as His instruments of judgment. In His sovereign control over history He could use such nations even without their knowledge. This proclamation had a major shaping effect on the messages of the prophets who came later.

The Concept of Amphictyony

Martin Noth suggested in the second quarter of this century that Israel's tribal organization during the period of the judges could best be described as an *amphictyony*. This was a term from ancient Greece describing a loose organization of people held together by a central sanctuary or worship center and a common cultus. For fifty years scholars used this concept to describe Israel's social and political organization during the Judges era. More thorough study in the last few years has shown that major differences exist between the Greek *amphictyony* and Israel's tribal organization. Thus both the idea and the term have fallen into disuse and need no further consideration. No other term has gained popular support to describe Israel's organization at this time. The Bible does not describe the political relationships of the tribes in this period. God was their Ruler. What human instruments and structures He used to exercise this rule, we do not know. Religious places such as Gilgal, Shiloh, Shechem, and Bethel were central. So were priests and judges. Worship, more than politics, provided the unifying factor.

Outline

The book of Judges picks up the narrative of Israel's history following the conquest under Joshua. It details the chaotic times that accompanied their transition from being conquering slaves into being a people settled in their own land. This outline will help in your study.

I. Israel's failures in securing the land (1:1—2:10)
   A. Tribal failures throughout the land (1:1–36)
   B. God's curse on the rebellion after Joshua (2:1–10)
II. The ministries of the judges (2:11—16:31)
   A. Summary of the era (2:11—3:6)
     1. The repetitive cycle (2:11–23)
     2. List of peoples in Canaan (3:1–6)
   B. The judgeship of Othniel (3:7–11)
   C. The judgeship of Ehud (3:12–30)
     1. Oppression by Moab (3:12–14)
     2. Eglon's assassination (3:15–25)
     3. Israel's victory (3:26–30)
   D. The judgeship of Shamgar (3:31)
   E. The judgeship of Deborah (4:1—5:31)
     1. Oppression by Jabin (4:1–3)
     2. Deborah confronts Barak (4:4–10)
     3. Victory over Sisera's army (4:12–16)
     4. Jael's murder of Sisera (4:11,17–22)
     5. Jabin's ultimate defeat (4:23–24)
     6. Deborah's song of victory (5:1–31)
   F. The judgeship of Gideon (6:1—8:35)
     1. The Midianite oppression (6:1–10)
     2. Gideon's call (6:11–40)
     3. Preparations (7:1–15)
     4. Israel's victory (7:16—8:21)
     5. Kingship rejected by Gideon (8:22–28)
     6. Apostasy renewed (8:29–35)
   G. Abimelech's abortive kingship (9:1–57)
   H. The judgeship of Tola (10:1–2)
   I. The judgeship of Jair (10:3–5)
   J. The judgeship of Jephthah (10:6—12:7)
     1. Rebellion and oppression (10:6–18)
     2. Jephthah's call (11:1–11)
     3. A rash vow and victory (11:12–33)
     4. Jephthah's daughter sacrificed (11:34–40)
     5. Ephraim's rebellion (12:1–7)
   K. The judgeship of Ibzan (12:8–10)
   L. The judgeship of Elon (12:11–12)

M. The judgeship of Abdon (12:13–15)

N. The judgeship of Samson (13:1—16:31)

1. Philistine oppression (13:1)

2. Birth of Samson (13:2–25)

3. Samson's love and its results (14:1—15:8)

4. Victory over the Philistines (15:9–20)

5. Samson's weakness and its consequences (16:1–21)

6. Samson's vengeance and self–sacrifice (16:22–31)

III. Dan's relocation and Benjamin's crisis (17:1—21:25)

A. Micah's idol (17:1–13)

B. Dan's involvements (18:1–31)

C. The outrage at Gibeah (19:1–21)

D. War with Benjamin (20:1–18)

E. Concern and provision for Benjamin (21:1–25)

Summary of Contents

The two narratives of Joshua and Judges partially overlap. Joshua ended with the death of its hero, but he was still alive during some of the initial events in Judges (Josh. 24:29–30; Judg. 2:6–7). This overlap provides evidence that although they were both apparently put into their final form by the Deuteronomic historians, they were initially the product of separate authors.

I. Israel's Failures in Securing the Land (1:1—2:10)

After the title verse (1:1), the narrative lists victories and defeats of the various tribes as they set about taking their allotments (1:2–36). Some victories appear, but we primarily find a long list of failures. The angel of the Lord announced to the people that their primary failure was in disobeying God (2:1–5). Their military failures resulted from their spiritual failure. Their final failure involved their children who were not led to covenant commitment to Yahweh. The tragic truth was that following the death of Joshua and the leaders who had served with him, "another generation grew up after them, who did not know the Lord or the work that he had done for Israel" (2:10). Thus the stage was set for the sad, tragic narrative of failure.

II. The Ministries of the Judges (2:11—16:31)

The information related to the minor judges is too brief to allow any real consideration of them here.

Othniel (1:13–15; 3:7–11) is described as a valiant warrior. He was raised up to defend his people against Cushan-rishathaim, a leader unmentioned outside the Bible. We may have his nickname instead of his name, for it can be translated as "Cushan of the double wickedness," that is one who was twice as bad as anyone else. The point is that when Israel rebelled against God, they faced someone who was twice as bad as themselves. When the people sought help, God delivered them from someone such as this.

The second, or according to some, the first of the major judges was **Ehud** (3:12–30). God raised up this left-handed judge to confront Eglon of Moab. He appeared before the king with Israel's tribute and with a secret message. This aroused the king's greed. This obese king apparently expected a bribe. The king, ever on guard, watched his enemy's right hand. Ehud had another surprise. He drew a dagger with his left hand, catching the king by surprise. The gruesome details of the king's death is a touch of horror characteristic of Judges.

Deborah is the only woman among the judges. Even one woman on the list is surprising in a patriarchal age. The Hebrew construction emphasizes her role as a *female* prophet (4:4). Even more surprising, she is shown to be far more heroic and faithful than Barak, the military leader of Israel's militia. Her story is told in a narrative (4:1–24) followed by a song of victory (5:1–31). The Song of Deborah is one of the older songs in the Bible.

The listing of the tribes and clans involved in the conflict (5:14–18) reveal that, though many were expected to participate, only a few shared any significant part of the conflict. The vivid description of the treachery of Jael and the brutal murder of Sisera once again strikes the horror typical of Judges. Finally, the description of the anxiety of Sisera's mother as she awaited her son's return from battle rings a responsive chord in the hearts of all who have seen loved ones go to war.

Gideon is introduced with humor. This may represent the author's attempt to relieve the tension built up in the narrative to this point (6:1—8:35). This reluctant hero was addressed as a brave man even though he was hiding in a wine press to thresh his wheat. This would normally have been done on a hilltop where the wind would blow the chaff away. Threshing grain on a hilltop would have invited the Midianites to see him and to plunder the grain. So Gideon, the hero being called to deliver his people, hid.

His confrontation by God led Gideon to prepare and purify his people for the task (6:17–35). Still fearful of what was before him, Gideon used the fleece text in an attempt to escape doing God's will. He already knew what God wanted, but he tried to present such an impossible situation that he might escape the responsibility. When God responded with a miracle, Gideon reversed the challenge, only to be foiled again (6:36–40). His reluctance overcome, he was commanded to reduce the size of his army. This forced him to rely on God instead of military might (7:1–8). The result was a victory over the marauding Midianites followed by his rejection of an attempt to crown him (7:9—8:28). God alone was Israel's king.

Unfortunately, Gideon's son, **Abimelech,** with the interesting name meaning "My father is king," was more ambitious, making an abortive attempt to become king of Israel (9:1–57). His plot, however, ultimately came to nothing, and the cycles of Israel's sin continued (10:6–16).

Jephthah, the next major judge, had been the victim of prejudice and ostracism because his mother was a harlot (11:1–4). In their desperation, however, the people of Gilead turned to him because of his obvious military skills. Jephthah foolishly pledged to sacrifice to God the first thing he met on his return after the battle (11:5–33). Sadly, the victim turned out to be his own daughter. Even more sadly, Jephthah blamed his daughter for his own folly, and we have a new stomach-turning point (11:34–40). Following Jephthah, apostate Israel once again regressed into their same old pattern of sin and rebellion (12:1—13:1).

Samson is the most familiar of the judges. We know parts of his story from its biblical detail and from its Hollywood reenactments. Four features of the story are most significant. First, after his miraculous birth his parents dedicated him to God for all of his life (13:2–25). The Hebrew word for "vow" is *nazir*, and so he was called a Nazirite. The outward symbol of being a Nazirite was that the hair was left uncut (Num. 6:2–8). Samson later obviously ignored this part of his life, but he never forgot it.

The second important aspect of Samson's life was his choice of a selfish playboy lifestyle. He ignored his parents, his people, and his God as he played around with the Philistines, his people's enemy, and gave himself over to self-gratification. God used him in spite of himself (14:1—16:19).

The third striking feature is the tragedy of his physical and spiritual downfall. The saddest verse of the Old Testament may be his statement when he awoke after Delilah's treachery: "I will go out as at other times, and shake myself free. *But he did not know that the Lord had left him"* (16:20, author's italics). He left God out of his life as he played around with sin, and he was not aware of God's abandonment.

The final important feature is that even at the end, he was more concerned with vengeance than with service, repentance, or forgiveness. God used His final act, but it was motivated by a desire for revenge.

III. Dan's Relocation and Benjamin's Crisis (17:1—21:35)

Judges draws to a close with two so-called appendices. While these two stories relating to the tribes of Dan and Benjamin carry on the narrative, they clearly do not relate to judges as we have seen them in the rest of the book.

Of all the tribes, only Dan did not take or maintain possession of the land God had given them. They were assigned territory adjacent to the Philistines in the Shephelah, but found it too difficult to control, so they sought out an easier region far to the north. In the process of turning down God's gift, they also got involved in idolatry, showing not only their rejection of God's gift, but their rejection of Yahweh (17:1—18:31).

The book's final story is perhaps the most revolting of all. An old man, seeking to protect the Levite visiting in his house from homosexual rape, offered his virgin daughter and the Levite's concubine to some of the men of Benjamin. When they refused to accept the offer, the Levite thrust his concubine out and locked the door. After she had been abused all night, the Levite cut her body into pieces and sent them throughout the tribes of Israel. This called the tribes to war against their own people, resulting in the tribe of Benjamin facing annihilation. Israel averted that fate by taking young women captive from Jabesh Gilead and providing them to the men of Benjamin (19:1—21:25). The entire episode was one of horror, selfishness, lust, and tragedy. Sadly, on this note Judges comes to an end.

Message

The proclamation of Judges seems to focus on two main points. The first concerns the sovereignty of Yahweh. In their sinful rebellion the people of Israel repeatedly revolted against God. Even their spiritual leaders were revolting. Yet God so controlled history and was so gracious that He could and did use such people to accomplish His ultimate purposes. That offers hope to us when we become aware of our sin and guilt.

The book's second major theme calls attention to Israel's state of spiritual and physical anarchy. Without a human king to lead them, the people did not appear able to stand before their neighbors who sought to destroy them. This is the foundation on which the story of Samuel and Kings is built. Out of the chaos of Israel's tribal existence, God was about to build His nation.

Questions for Review and Reflection

1. What is the major theme of the Book of Judges?
2. Name the persons whom God raised up as Israel's judges. What was the role of the judge?
3. Do you believe in a cyclic view of history? Why or why not?
4. How is fertility related to religion? What answer did Israel have for the fertility cult worshipers?
5. Were all the judges heroes? Why were the exploits of people like Abimelech and Samson included in the Book of Judges?

Bibliography

Boling, Robert G. Judges: *A New Translation with Notes and Commentary.* Vol. 6A of *Anchor Bible,* Garden City: Doubleday, 1975.

Gray, John. *Joshua, Judges, Ruth. (New Century Bible Commentary).* Grand Rapids: William B. Eerdmans, 1986.

Hamlin, E. John. *At Risk in the Promise Land: A commentary on the book of Judges.* Grand Rapids: Eerdmans, 1990.

Soggin, J. Alberto. *Judges: A Commentary.* in *International Theological Commentary.* Philadelphia: Westminster Press, 1981.

Chapter 4

The Book of Ruth

The Book of Ruth is one of the world's great literary master-pieces. Simple, well written, and with an appeal that touches the hardest or most insensitive heart, Ruth communicates with people where they live. While focusing on human tragedy and loss of hope, it presents a love that will not give up and that ultimately wins out. Throughout the major plot, several subplots are interwoven superbly.

Place in the Canon, Date, and Authorship

Ruth does not follow Judges and is not a part of the Former Prophets in the Hebrew canon. It is located in the Writings (Hebrew: *Kethubim),* a collection of five short books called the *Megilloth,* a term meaning "rolls" or "scrolls".[1] These five books, or scrolls, were each read aloud at one of the major Jewish festivals or fasts. They are Song of Songs, read at Passover; Ruth, read at Pentecost; Lamentations, read at the Fast on the ninth of Ab; Ecclesiastes, read at Tabernacles; and Esther, read at Purim. These five books have no other literary or historical connection to one

---

1. The nature of the Megilloth as a collection is seldom dealt with by Old Testament writers and at least offers a possibility for fruitful investigations. A brief introduction to the collection is found in James King West's *Introduction to the Old Testament* (Macmillan Publishing Co., 1981, second ed.), 462–69.

another. Ruth's location alerts us that the ancient Hebrews perceived Ruth to be different from the six books that make up the Former Prophets.

GLOSSARY	
Writings	The third section of the Hebrew Scriptures.
Megilloth	Hebrew term for the five scrolls read at different annual Israelite religious festivals and fasts: Ruth, Lamentations, Esther, Ecclesiastes, Song of Solomon.
Levirate	Hebrew legal custom that called on the closest survivor of a deceased husband to marry the widow, provide a son to carry on the family name, tradition, and inheritance, and protect the family land claims. See Deuteronomy 25:5–10; Matthew 22:23–33.
Go'el	Hebrew term meaning "redeemer" and referring to person who assumed protective role for the helpless, especially the relative who assumed Levirate responsibilities and the person who avenged wrong against the family or tribe. See Genesis 38:8; Exodus 21:12–13; Leviticus 25:25–48; Numbers 35:6–34; Deuteronomy 4:41–43; 19:1–13; Joshua 20:1–9.[2]
Gleaner	Poor person or alien who gathered grain or produce the original harvesters missed. See Leviticus 19:9–10; 23:22; Deuteronomy 24:19–21; Isaiah 17:5–9; 27:12).
Kethubim	The Hebrew name for the third major division of the Old Testament canon, meaning "The Writings." This section is also known by its Latin name of Hagiographa, which means "Wise Writings."

---

2. A brief but informative survey of the Old Testament's understanding of God as Redeemer can be found in Robert L. Cate, *Old Testament Roots for New Testament Faith* (Broadman, 1982), 182–89.

Ruth was placed after Judges in the Septuagint (LXX), the earliest Greek translation of the Old Testament, since its setting was "In the days when the judges ruled" (Ruth 1:1). Jerome's Latin Vulgate continued this positioning and was followed by the earliest English translators.

An ancient Hebrew tradition identifies Samuel as its author, but since we have neither internal nor external evidence to indicate its human author, most Bible students today admit that the author of Ruth is unknown.

Although the book is clearly set in the time of the Judges, the date of its actual writing is debated. Some scholars assign it to the period of the judges, others to the time of Ezra and Nehemiah, and a few seek a middle ground in the era of the Hebrew monarchy.

Those who consider Ruth to be written late offer these reasons. (1) Ruth is located in the Writings, the last part of the Hebrew Bible to be canonized. (2) Several Aramaisms are found, and the first use of Aramaic in the Bible is in the priestly-Levitical histories that include Ezra and Nehemiah. (3) Ruth portrays life in Palestine as being rather serene, a far cry from how it is portrayed in Judges. (4) Customs practiced in the era of the judges seem to have been long abandoned and have to be explained. (5) Its message seems most appropriate to the plight of post-exilic Israel, with Boaz representing the Jews left in Palestine, Naomi the returning exiles, and Ruth the foreigners who came along with the exiles. Out of the relationship of these three had come Israel's great Kingdom under David, so the three groups could together be used by God to establish His new kingdom of peace.

Those supporting the early date point to other evidence. (1) Ruth's place in the Writings may have been due to its sanction of foreign marriages and nothing more. (2) The serene environment could have been characteristic of Bethlehem at some limited time during this period. (3) Explanations of earlier practices could have been added later by scribes for clarification. (4) The literary style of Ruth is more similar to 1 and 2 Samuel than to any other part of the Bible.

Interpreters supporting the monarchical date seem more concerned to find a compromise between the two extremes than with any hard evidence for their view. No scholarly consensus exists, nor is one likely to appear.

The book is one of the literary masterpieces of the world. Based on a series of rather insignificant historical events, this love story communicates with all who read it. At the same time, it gently proclaims the sovereign love of a God who works out His purposes in people's lives even when they are unaware of it.

Organization of the Book

Ruth has only a general chronological setting, "In the days when the judges ruled" (1:1). Its geographical and emotional settings are more precise. It deals with a family from Bethlehem who fled to Moab in a time of famine. Tragedy struck. The father and two sons died. Naomi, the lone survivor, returned home to a life of poverty, accompanied by a widowed daughter-in-law, Ruth. The book tells the story of the many dimensions of Ruth's love, devotion, and loyalty, which together resulted in establishing the line of David and eventually produced David's greater Son. The development of the story may be followed by this outline.

    I.   Flight to and sojourn in Moab (1:1–5)

    II.   The grieving return to Bethlehem (1:6–22)

    III.   A struggle with poverty (2:1–23)

    IV.   Ruth's daring boldness (3:1–18)

    V.   Redemption by Boaz (4:1–12)

    VI.   The line of David (4:13–22)

Summary of Contents

If the book of Ruth were not found in the Bible, its simple love story would place it on the best seller list among the world's great love stories. Ruth's profound presentation of the various dimensions of human love and devotion stir the most hardened heart. It is unique in the literature of the ancient Near East and of the Bible in featuring two women as its central figures.

I. Flight to and Sojourn in Moab (1:1–5)

The story begins as a tragedy with a famine in Bethlehem (1:1). This must have been a severe famine, for Bethlehem means "House of Bread." It was actually the major supplier of grain (bread) for the entire land. As a consequence of the famine, Naomi, her husband, and her two sons fled for refuge to Moab, one of Israel's bitter enemies. There tragedy multiplied for Naomi, for her husband died, then her two sons married foreign women and subsequently died.

II. The Grieving Return to Bethlehem (1:6–22)

In the midst of her grief and bereavement, Naomi decided to return home to Bethlehem, urging both daughters-in-law to remain behind. Only after a second urging did Orpah do so. Ruth, however, refused. Instead she uttered a commitment that stands among the world's great declarations of love and fidelity:

> Do not press me to leave you
> or to turn back from following you!
> Where you go, I will go;
> Where you lodge, I will lodge;
> your people shall be my people,
> and your God my God.
> Where you die, I will die—
> there will I be buried.
> (1:16–17)

In making this promise, Ruth traded her national citizenship for that of an alien among enemies. She swapped her home and family for the companionship of a bitter, barren woman and gave up her religion for a God who supported enemy armies. She surrendered even her family burial ground, a plot of major importance for people of the ancient Near East. Unfortunately, Naomi in her grief appreciated none of this. She arrived at Bethlehem bitterly protesting to her welcoming friends that she was returning "empty," neither acknowledging nor even recognizing that Ruth was there to comfort and sustain her.

III. A Struggle with Poverty (2:1–23)

In a day when only men had legal rights, Ruth and Naomi, with no man to protect nor care for them, were forced to live in abject poverty. Daily existence became a struggle. Simply to survive, Ruth was forced to become a gleaner. We do not know if Naomi was too old or too incapacitated by grief to share in this task. In any case, Ruth did the gleaning alone. During this time, Boaz noticed Ruth, apparently being attracted by her beauty and devotion. As a consequence, he befriended her, offering her not only extra grain but protection and food as well.

IV. Ruth's Daring Boldness (3:1–18)

Naomi, perhaps beginning to overcome her grief, realized that Boaz was a kinsman of her late husband, Elimelech (2:3; 3:2). Not only were family ties important in ancient Israel, legal obligations went along with them. The nearest of kin bore the special responsibility of being a *go'el* or "redeemer." One part of this responsibility was that of Levirate marriage (Deut. 25:5–10). When a man died without a male heir, the nearest of kin inherited the legal responsibility to marry the widow of the deceased. The first male child of that union was considered to be the legal heir of the deceased so that the deceased "lived on" in Israel. This assured that his inheritance remained within the family and clan. Further, the *go'el* was also expected to buy or "redeem" the land of the deceased to keep it in the family.

Recognizing the forgotten possibilities of such a relationship, Naomi urged Ruth to lay her claim on Boaz. Ruth responded with gentle boldness. Her act of faith was laden with danger. At the very least she could have been rejected. At the worst she could have been abused. Already attracted to Ruth, Boaz acknowledged his responsibility. One problem! Boaz stood second in line. A closer relative had a prior obligation.

V. Redemption by Boaz (4:1–12)

The narrator's silence provides a bit of humor and romance. Boaz did not allow the other man to see Ruth during the subsequent negotiations. First, Boaz laid the responsibility and opportunity of purchasing Elimelech's property before the other man. Then he added, as a seeming after thought, that marriage with a foreign woman went along with the deal. This quickly dampened the enthusiasm of the other man, who eagerly turned over both responsibilities to Boaz.

VI. The Line of David (4:13–22)

Ruth and Boaz were married. From that union came a son, Obed, who later became the grandfather of Israel's greatest king, David. Further, from that line eventually came David's greater Son, Jesus. Ruth, the hated foreigner, joined four other women in the official list of Jesus' ancestors (Matt. 1:1–16). Naomi, who had returned bitter and distraught, now had a home in which to live and grandchildren to love and nurture. Thus God used what others considered foreign or pagan to accomplish His ultimate purposes of redemption.

Message

The theological message of this little book has a profundity far beyond its size. The overarching theme appears to be that the sovereign love of a sovereign God can and does accomplish His purposes even in the midst of human tragedy. He can and does redeem the worst situations and the most improbable people in accomplishing those purposes. Further, on a human level, we are pointed to the fact that foreign pagans can and often do demonstrate greater loyalty and greater love than the so-called "people of God."

Ruth as an Individual

Ruth is one of the truly great people in the Bible. This minority, alien woman did not rebel against her lot in life. As a woman in a patriarchal society, her identity and rights were largely dependent on belonging to a male. This had been her father until she had risked everything in crossing racial, cultural, and national barriers to marry a Hebrew. When her husband died, she was totally bereft. Her only hope of reestablishing her identity would have been to return to her father's house with the ultimate hope of marrying a man of her own people.

Ruth showed that her compassion was greater than her self-interest. She chose to accompany and care for her bereft mother-in-law, whom she apparently perceived to be in greater need than herself. Doing this meant giving up everything—her home, her family, her nationality, her friends, and her god, Chemosh of the Moabites. She showed she was not afraid of hard work nor of risk and danger.

Finally, God chose Ruth in His grace to have a major place both in the history of the Hebrew kingdom and in the history of His ultimate plan of redemption. In fulfilling her obligations as she saw them, Ruth did far more than anyone would ever have asked or expected. In accepting her lot with grace, love, and courage, she was allowed to play a part in Hebrew, Christian, and world history beyond her or anyone else's wildest imaginations.

Questions for Review and Reflection

1. What emotions must Ruth and Naomi have felt when news of death reached them? How did they each respond? Did the responses show that one was a better person or closer to God than the other? Why?

2. What factors influenced Naomi's request of her daughters-in-law? What caused the different responses?

3. What is the basic teaching you get from reading the Book of Ruth? What literary features make it a masterpiece of world literature?

4. To what current situations does the Book of Ruth speak?

Bibliography

Cate, Robert L. *Discovering Judges, Ruth, 1 and 2 Samuel.* Carmel: Guideposts, 1988.

Enns, Paul P. Ruth, *A Bible Study Commentary.* Grand Rapids: Zondervan, 1982.

Hubbard, Robert L. *Ruth.* New International Commentary on the Old Testament. Grand Rapids: Eerdmans, 1988.

Kennedy, J. Hardee. *Ruth.* In vol. 2 The Broadman Bible CommentaryNashville: Broadman Press, 1970.

Sasson, Jack M. *Ruth.* Baltimore: The John Hopkins University Press.1979.

Chapter 5

The Books of 1 and 2 Samuel

With the Books of 1 and 2 Samuel, we have arrived at the origin of the Hebrew monarchy. Samuel, the last of the judges, and Saul and David, the first two Hebrew kings, dominate the narrative. The claim of being the first king of Israel goes to Saul. David, however, gets the credit for actually establishing the Hebrew monarchy on a solid basis. For the rest of Israel's history, David remained the symbol of Israel's greatness. His was Israel's golden age. He is the central figure of 1 and 2 Samuel.

Glossary	
Ark of God	The chest made to contain the Ten Commandments, along with other symbols of God's providential concern for His people. It was placed in the center of the most holy place first in the tabernacle, then in the temple.
Book of Jashar	An ancient book or scroll of Hebrew war songs, some of which are quoted in the Old Testament.

Glossary	
City of David	A common nickname for Jerusalem, since it was technically outside of the territory controlled by the Hebrews until David conquered it and made it his capital.
Elegy	A song or poem of mourning and grief.
Prophet	A spokesman for God, proclaiming His message to the chosen people. Prophets were more often forth-tellers rather than fore-tellers, seeking to apply God's words to their people in their immediate present.
Shiloh	The shrine at which Samuel ministered and which apparently served as Israel's central place of worship during the period of the judges and the early days of the monarchy.

Place in the Canon, Date, and Authorship

The Books of 1 and 2 Samuel bring us back to the Hebrew canon's Former Prophets section that began with Joshua. These are two of the six books scholars have identified as the Deuteronomic history. (See chap. 1 section on "The Books to Be Covered.") In studying these books, we should look for similarity in language and teaching to Deuteronomy as we determine the message proclaimed through the events recorded.

First and Second Samuel were written as one book. Later scribes divided them into two, probably because their contents were too long for one scroll. The dividing point between the two books is quite artificial. First Samuel ends with the death of Saul, but David's response to Saul's death is given in 2 Samuel 1. These books also seem to be one with 1 and 2 Kings, for the division between 2 Samuel and 1 Kings appears just as artificial. David's reign is drawing to a close at the end of 2 Samuel, but his death is not actually reported until 1 Kings.

The Septuagint translators about 200 B.C. designated the four books as 1, 2, 3, and 4 Kingdoms. Whether they introduced the separation into four books or made the separation, we cannot determine. In producing the Latin Vulgate, Jerome shortened these

titles to 1, 2, 3, and 4 Kings. This evidence shows an ongoing relationships between all four of these books, but obvious differences
should show that the process of writing probably involved several
different people over an extended time.

The authorship of 1 and 2 Samuel was traditionally ascribed
to Samuel. The report of Samuel's death early in the narrative (1
Sam. 25:1; 28:3) makes this highly unlikely. Tradition attached
Samuel's name to the books probably because they deal primarily
with the establishment of the Hebrew kingdom, in which Samuel
played a major part. Most likely, Samuel was responsible for some
of the material in 1 Samuel. Much later, the author of 1 and 2
Chronicles identified Samuel as one source of his material, although his reference is obviously not to our biblical Books of Samuel.

> Now the acts of King David, from first to last, are written in the
> records of the seer Samuel, and in the records of the prophet Nathan,
> and in the records of the seer Gad, with accounts of all his rule and his
> might and the events that befell him and Israel and all the kingdoms of
> the earth. (1 Chron. 29:29–30)

Clearly, if such records were available to the Chronicler, they
were available to the writer of 1 and 2 Samuel.

The author of 1 and 2 Samuel cited the Book of Jashar as the
source of David's elegy over the deaths of Saul and Jonathan (2
Sam 1:18). Note that this source was also quoted in Joshua 10:13.
The Septuagint of 1 Kings 8:12–13 apparently refers to this source
although textual changes have blurred this reference.[1] The author clearly found no difficulty in turning to other sources for the
material from which he gathered his information. This should not
be surprising, for no one person could have lived through all of
these events and over this expanse of time.

A number of interpreters think that they have identified two
basic sources in the Books of Samuel. These are normally identified as the early, or eyewitness account, and a later one, revealing
further reflection on the meaning of the events. The contention
is made that the earlier source viewed the kingship from a favorable position, used excellent Hebrew, and vividly described events
in a way that captured the imagination of the readers. According

---

1. See "Jashar," in *The Interpreter's Dictionary of the Bible* (Abingdon Press,
1962), vol. 2, 803; Duane Christensen, "Jashar, Book of," The Anchor Bible Dictionary 3 (New York: Doubleday, 1992), 646-47.

to this theory, the so-called later source used poorer Hebrew, was critical of the kingship, and pronounced Deuteronomy's judgment on it.

Those who support this position point to the large number of apparent duplicate reports of the same events that are found here.

1. The end of Eli's family is twice predicted (1 Sam. 2:31–36; 3:11–14).
2. Saul's anointing as king was held twice publicly and once privately (1 Sam. 9:26—10:1; 10:17–24; 11:15).
3. The origin of the proverb, "Is Saul also among the prophets?" is twice reported (1 Sam. 10:11; 19:24).
4. Although deposed from his throne twice, Saul continued to reign until his death (1 Sam. 13:14; 15:26–29).
5. On two occasions David was introduced to Saul (1 Sam. 16:14–23; 17:55–58).
6. Goliath was slain once by David and once by Elhanan. The Chronicler apparently used this information later to report that Elhanan killed Goliath's brother (1 Sam. 17; 19:5; 21:9; 22:10*b*, 13; 2 Sam. 21:19; 1 Chr. 20:5).
7. David made three different covenants with Jonathan (1 Sam. 18:3; 20:16–42; 23:18).
8. On three occasions David was offered a daughter of King Saul in marriage (1 Sam. 18:17–19, 20–21*a*, 22*b*–29*a*).
9. David twice fled from Saul's court never to return (1 Sam. 19:12; 20:42*b*).
10. Saul was immediately aware of David's first flight; however, he later wondered why he was not present at the king's feast (1 Sam. 19:17; 20:25–29).
11. David twice sought refuge from Achish of Gath (1 Sam. 21:10–15; 27:1–4).
12. Treason on the part of the Ziphites is twice reported (1 Sam. 23:19–28; 26:1).
13. On two occasions, David had Saul in his power and spared his life (1 Sam. 24:3–7; 26:5–12).
14. Saul is reported to have died in two different ways (1 Sam. 31:4; 2 Sam. 1:6–10).
15. Absalom is reported to have had three sons, yet later is said to have had no son (2 Sam. 14:27; 18:18).

Each of these so-called dual accounts can be explained satisfactorily. On the other hand, the multiplicity of them when coupled with the other evidence of possible sources behind 1 and 2 Samuel make such a suggestion possible. That there may have been two major sources along with the other suggested sources creates no real problems. No one questions the validity of four Gospels to present the life of Jesus. We may simply have had a similar situation here, except they have been woven together by an editor, possibly the Deuteronomic historian(s).

Serious students of these books also seek to identify the date of their final compilation. First, we need to recognize that the possibility of multiple sources does not militate against the sources being contemporaneous with one another. One does not have to be early and another late. The explanation of archaic sayings and outdated customs seems to indicate that the final editing was completed long after the events were recorded (1 Sam. 9:9; 2 Sam. 13:18). In addition, the phrase, "to this day," is used repeatedly to refer to past events whose effects were still being felt long afterwards (1 Sam. 5:5; 6:18; 27:6; 30:25; 2 Sam. 4:3; 6:8; 18:18).

Adding strength to this conclusion is the fact that the entire length of David's reign is reported shortly after he assumed the kingship, even though his death is not even recorded in these books (1 Kings 2:10). The final piece of evidence is a reference to the kings of Judah, a reference that would have been meaningless until at least the reigns of two or more kings following the division at Solomon's death (1 Sam. 27:6). We are forced to conclude that 1 and 2 Samuel could not have been finished any earlier than the third reign in the kingdom of Judah. The books were probably completed nearer the time of Josiah or even in the period of the exile if the final editing joined Samuel to the Books of Kings.

Organization

Since the main story of 1 and 2 Samuel develops around the three figures of Samuel, Saul, and David, their prominence is pointed out in the outline points. Although the outline covers both books, I have only identified the specific book in the outline section where the division between the two overlap the narrative.

I. Samuel brings the era of the judges to an end (1 Sam. 1:1–8:3)

A. Samuel's birth and dedication (1:1—2:11)

      B. The failure and rejection of Eli (2:12–36)

      C. Samuel's call and subsequent ministry (3:1—8:3)

  II. Samuel initiates the Hebrew kingdom by anointing Saul (1 Sam. 8:4—10:27)

      A. Israel's plea for a king (8:4–22)

      B. Saul anointed as king (9:1—10:27)

  III. Saul's early reign over Israel (1 Sam. 11:1—15:35)

      A. Saul's first days as king (11:1—12:25)

      B. Saul's difficulties, failures, victories, defeats, and rejection (13:1—15:35)

  IV. Saul's later reign over Israel with David's increasing popularity (1 Sam. 16:1—22:23)

      A. David anointed a future king (16:1–13)

      B. David enters Saul's service (16:14–23)

      C. David overcomes Goliath (17:1–58)

      D. David's successes and Saul's jealousy (18:1–30)

      E. David flees from Saul's anger (19:1—22:23)

  V. David's actions in Saul's last days (1 Sam. 23:1—30:31)

      A. David's continued conflict with Saul (23:1—24:22)

      B. David's weakness with women (25:1–43)

      C. David flees to the Philistines (26:1—30:31)

  VI. David's response to the deaths of Saul and Jonathan (1 Sam 31:1—2 Sam. 1:27)

      A. Deaths of Saul and Jonathan (2 Sam. 31:1–13)

      B. David's act of vengeance (1:1–16)

      C. David's lament (1:17–27)

  VII. David reigns over Judah (2 Sam. 2:1—4:12)

      A. David anointed king over Judah (2:1–4*a*)

      B. David's relations with Israel (2:4*b*—4:12)

  VIII. David's early reign over Israel (2 Sam. 5:1—10:19)

      A. David anointed at Hebron (5:1–5)

      B. David seizes Jerusalem for his capital (5:6—7:29)

      C. David's victories (8:1—10:19)

  IX. David's personal problems (2 Sam. 11:1—18:33)

      A. David and Bathsheba (11:1—12:31)

      B. Amnon rapes Tamar (13:1–19)

C. Absalom's vengeance (13:20–39)

D. Absalom's return and rebellion (14:1—18:33)

X. David's final days as king (2 Sam. 19:1—24:25)

A. David returns with acts of mercy (19:1–43)

B. Days of turbulence (20:1—21:22)

C. David's last songs (22:1—23:7)

D. David's administrative successes and failures (23:8—24:17)

Summary of Contents

Judges ended on a note of pathos, "In those days there was no king in Israel" (Judg. 18:1; 19:1; 21:25). The Books of 1 and 2 Samuel overlap this era and carry on the narrative, reporting how the kingdom got its start. The entire narrative revolves around the activities and inter-relations of the three central figures: Samuel, the last of the judges; Saul, the first king; and David, the second and greatest king Israel ever had.

I. Samuel Brings the Era of the Judges to an End (1 Sam. 1:1—8:3)

The narrative of 1 Samuel begins with the story of Hannah's childlessness and the miraculous birth of her son, Samuel (1:1—2:10). In ancient Israel, people seldom raised the issue of life after death. For most people, their basic hope of "immortality" was to live on in the family line, thus maintaining a relationship with the covenant community and with the covenant God. This necessitated a male child to carry on the family. A childless woman brought a sense of despair and hopelessness to herself and her husband. Hannah's heartache at her plight can only be fully sensed when this is understood and appreciated.

Hannah's prayer for a son brought a strange response from Eli, the priest at Shiloh. Seeing the woman agonizing silently, he said with disgust, "How long will you make a drunken spectacle of yourself? Put away your wine" (1 Sam. 1:14). Eli's assumption that she was drunk rather than praying is surprising. It underscores the tragedy of which we learn later: Eli's sons were worthless men, even bringing prostitutes into the holy worship place (1 Sam. 2:12–17,22).

Following his weaning, customarily between the child's third and fourth birthdays, Samuel was turned over to Eli to serve him at the shrine of Shiloh. Although Eli had failed as a father, he served as Samuel's mentor, guiding him into recognizing and accepting Yahweh's call. Young Samuel was given an amazing responsibility in his call, that of announcing the absolute downfall of Eli, a man who obviously meant a great deal to him. The end result of Samuel's call was that God's word was once again heard in Israel, as the people listened to and received the words of Samuel (1 Sam. 3:1—4:1a).

Throughout the remainder of this section, Samuel is shown fulfilling the combined offices of prophet, priest, and judge (1 Sam. 3:20; 7:6,15–18). As a judge, he served both as a charismatic leader and as a judicial mediator, hearing cases and rendering decisions. As a priest, he erected an altar and offered sacrifice. As a prophet, he spoke the words of Yahweh to the people.

Many interpreters of the Old Testament speak as if prophets and priests were always in conflict. That is not so. Frequently they worked together toward the same goals and often, as here, the offices were filled by the same person.

The major focus of Israel's history during this part of Samuel's life and ministry was their ongoing conflict with the Philistines.[2] During that conflict, the people of Israel took the ark of God to the battle with them, due to a popular belief that God was in some way always localized over or around it. They were trying to force Him to fight their battles. Unfortunately, their view of God was too small.

In the ancient Near East and in Israel at this time, most people believed that a victory over a people was a victory over their god(s). The Philistines and Israel discovered in these battles that this was simply not so. Israel was defeated, but the gods of the Philistine confederation were powerless before Yahweh. He ultimately had the victory. (Unfortunately, this was a lesson not long remembered.)

---

2. The Philistine offered a major problem to the people of Israel for an extended period. A thorough study may be found in R. A. Kitchen, "The Philistines," in *Peoples of Old Testament Times* (Clarendon Press, 1973), and T. Dothan and M. Dothan, *People of the Sea: The Search for the Philistines* (New York: MacMillan, 1992); T. Dothan, *The Philistines and Their Material Culture* (New Haven: Yale University Press, 1982); D. Howard, The Philistines, *Peoples of the Old Testament World*, ed. A. Hoerth, G. Mattingly, and E. Yamaguchi (Grand Rapids: Baker, 1993).

The fact that the Philistines returned the captured ark with an offering of golden tumors and mice has been interpreted as indicating that they suffered from an outbreak of the bubonic plague. Fleas on mice are the carriers of the disease that produces an outbreak of tumors on the sufferer.

Samuel failed at the same point as had Eli, his mentor. They both failed as fathers. Samuel's sons did not follow in his faith. He appointed them judges over Israel in spite of this (1 Sam. 8:1–3). Obviously, a father cannot be held totally responsible for the failure of his sons; but he need not pretend that everything is all right and that the sons are qualified to carry on his ministry. All who are parents need to be warned that they can become so involved in ministry to others that they fail to minister to the family for whom they are most responsible.

II. Samuel Initiates the Hebrew Kingdom by Anointing Saul (1 Sam. 8:4—10:27)

The elders of Israel finally approached Samuel with a startling request: "Appoint for us, then, a king to govern us, like other nations" (8:5). This was a startling request, particularly coming from people who so deeply treasured their independence. Their request was based on four factors. First, while Samuel had been a reasonably effective leader, his sons were failures. The people did not want them succeeding their father (8:5). Their second reason was their desire "to be like all the nations." They were tired of being different. Their third reason was rooted and grounded in the second. They recognized that they could not continue to exist with everyone doing what was right in his own eyes. They needed someone "to govern" them (8:5, 20). When they got to the fourth reason, they were probably expressing what was uppermost in their minds. They wanted a king to "go out before us and fight our battles" (8:20). The Israelites were frightened of the Philistines, realized that an organized national army was needed, and recognized that an organized army required someone to be in command.

Obviously distressed by the elders' request, Samuel voiced his concern in prayer. Yahweh's response granted the request of the people. It also revealed that Samuel's biggest distress centered on what he had perceived to be Israel's rejection of his own leadership. He had to be reminded that the people had not rejected Samuel, they had rejected God. As at Sinai and again in Canaan, the Hebrews were still having trouble maintaining confidence in a God they could not see. They wanted someone with authority nearer by.[3]

Although God granted their request, He also clearly wanted the people to be aware of the ultimate cost (8:10–18). God never allows His people to make decisions blindly. Because the people persisted in their demands, God initiated the process by which Saul was chosen as Israel's first king.

Saul is introduced as a young man who was outstanding in those characteristics that attract human admiration. A man of wealth and extremely handsome, he possessed an outstanding physique (9:1–2). A hard worker who sought to fulfill his responsibilities, he remained modest and filled with humility (9:3–4,21). After he was anointed king, he proved to be both patient and generous with those who objected to his being king. He finally attracted the support of many of the people (10:27).

Two events in the process pointed to potential future problems for Saul and Israel. First, Saul's becoming a part of the ecstatic frenzy of a roving band of prophets may have indicated an unstable personality. Such bands were fairly common in the ancient Near East. Second, Saul's hiding when the time of the final coronation came may have indicated either extreme timidity or a sense of inadequacy. Either characteristic is potentially dangerous for one who leads in critical times. The pause to search for Saul upstaged Samuel's dramatic moment. This may have been the basis for future bad relations between the two. Israel moved historically from the period of the judges to that of the monarchy. They had a king and, unfortunately, Israel had become *like all the nations.*

III. Saul's Early Reign over Israel (1 Sam. 11:1—15:35)

Saul's first significant act as king of Israel was to rescue the people of Jabesh-Gilead by defeating the besieging Ammonites (11:1–11). The people of Israel were excited by this, for it fulfilled the precise reason they had wanted a king in the first place. The immediate response of some was a desire to execute those who had opposed Saul's kingship (11:12–13). Saul refused to allow

---

3. The covenant itself had identified Yaweh as the King of Israel. See Robert L. Cate, *Old Testament Roots for New Testament Faith* (Broadman, 1982), 116–27 (esp. 122). For a review of the meaning of covenant, see Trent C. Butler, "Covenant" *Holman Bible Dictionary* (Nashville: Holman Bible Publishers, 1991), 308-12.

this, being merciful to his enemies, an act that further endeared him to his people.

Samuel intervened at this point, reaffirming Saul in the kingship and leading Israel in a service of thanksgiving to God for victory (11:14–15). Samuel, however, apparently could not stand Saul's initial success, so he warned Israel once again of their apostasy in wanting a king. This did nothing to add to Saul's self-confidence (12:1–25). Samuel's main emphasis was a call on both Israel and their king to be faithful and loyal to Yahweh. Blessing would follow obedience. Defeat and destruction would follow rebellion. The themes of Deuteronomy remained valid.

Samuel's warning is followed by a fascinating yet confusing statement. "Saul was . . . years old when he began to reign; and he reigned . . . and two years over Israel" (13:1). The two gaps in the manuscript show just how carefully the ancient scribes sought to preserve the texts they received. Obviously something is missing, and many modern translators have tried to supply the missing numbers. When ancient scribes received a text in which an insect or a mouse had eaten a hole, they refused the temptation to correct it and passed it on just as it had been received.

Saul's reign featured a mixture of successes and failures. He met the people's needs by winning battles for them, but conflict with Samuel heated up. When Saul marched to battle with the Philistines, Samuel failed to show up to offer sacrifices. Terrified that idle soldiers might desert him, Saul offered the sacrifice himself. Samuel, who may have been waiting nearby to see what Saul would do, suddenly showed up and condemned Saul for his foolish haste.[4] While Saul clearly sinned, Samuel's delay put undue pressure on Saul's growing sense of insecurity.

Samuel informed Saul that because he disobeyed God's command, God had rejected him as king of Israel (13:2–14).

An editorial note appears at this point (13:19–23). Israel faced a severe disadvantage in their conflict with the Philistines because they could not produce iron weapons. This almost sounds modern. From a human perspective, Israel could explain their defeats. The balance of power had been unbalanced because Israel trailed in this ancient arms race.

---

4. We do not know all that was involved here. At a later time both David and Solomon did similar things with no priestly opposition. (2 Sam 6:12–19; 24:25; 1 Kings 3:15) Obviously, there was something involved here which the original readers understood but of which we no longer know.

Saul's oath and Jonathan's unwitting disobedience indicates again the seriousness with which ancient Israel regarded the spoken word (14:1–46). Had not the people redeemed Jonathan out of Saul's hand, the king would have executed his own son.

Despite Samuel's threat, Saul continued to reign and won a series of victories over Israel's enemies. Even as his spiritual might waned, his military might increased (14:47–52). He again revealed his weakness. Trying to cover up his inadequacies or to show piety before the people, Saul flagrantly disobeyed God in his victory over the Amalekites (15:1–9). In response, Samuel confronted Saul with one of the great proclamations in the Old Testament:

> Has the Lord as great delight in
> burnt offerings and sacrifices,
> as in obeying the voice of the Lord?
> Surely, to obey is better than sacrifice,
> and to heed than the fat of rams.
> For rebellion is no less a sin than divination,
> and stubbornness is like iniquity and idolatry.
> Because you have rejected the
> word of the Lord,
> he has also rejected you from being king.
> (1 Sam. 15:22–23)

Though neither Saul nor Samuel knew it, this was the last time they would ever see each other. Their relationship had been quite complex. Neither seemed to have loved nor respected the other. Still, when God revealed to Samuel that He had rejected Saul, the prophet pleaded with God all night long (15:11). The insecure Saul was forced to face the end of his reign without the support and encouragement of the man of God. The breach between these two leaders had to have been obvious to the people of Israel, only accentuating the insecurity of the king.

IV. Saul's Later Reign over Israel with David's Increasing Popularity (1 Sam. 16:1–22:23)

With Yahweh's rejection of Saul, Israel needed a new leader. Chiding Samuel for the inactivity of his grief, God sent him out to find His new choice. Grief often paralyzes. A step toward dealing with grief is action. Samuel sought for and found God's new king among the sons of Jesse. To Samuel and to Jesse, David the shepherd was an unlikely choice (16:1–13). However unlikely David was, he was God's choice.

Israel had a reigning king who had been rejected and a non-serving king who was yet to be crowned. To further complicate the situation, "the spirit of the Lord departed from Saul, and an evil spirit from the Lord tormented him" (16:14). This statement troubles modern interpreters. The idea of God sending an evil spirit does not fit our concept of God. Israel's conviction that God was ultimately sovereign meant that whatever happened ultimately came from God. Only later in their developing understanding of secondary causes did they ascribe such unhappy visitations as coming from Satan (compare 2 Sam. 24:1; 1 Chron. 21:1). Even then God remained sovereign over Satan. In a strange twist, Saul's torment finally found solace only in the musical talents of David, God's yet unrevealed choice to succeed him (16:15–23).

Saul's troubles were more than personal. His nation faced more pressure from the Philistine power. History's stage appeared set for the ultimate confrontation. Philistines put forward their champion and challenged Israel to send forth theirs, winner take all. No Israelite, not even Saul or Jonathan, dared to accept the challenge. Then shepherd boy David appeared with food for his soldier brothers. Incensed at the audacity of Goliath and the timidity of the soldiers of God's army, David volunteered to confront the giant (17:1–32).

Interpreters frequently misunderstand one detail of that battle. They picture David as a little boy when he was already a mature youth, a competent shepherd who had bravely and victoriously confronted wild animals that attacked his sheep. When he offered his royal armor to David, Saul was not trying to make him look ridiculous. He was trying to equip him for a dangerous battle. Saul was taller than anyone in his army, and David was apparently close to the same size (8:2). David did not turn down Saul's offer because the armor did not fit, but because he was not familiar with its use (17:39). David killed Goliath, the Philistines fled in dismay, and Israel was victorious.

The people of Israel welcomed the victorious Hebrews back from the battle, singing victory songs about David's exploits (18:6–7). This further increased Saul's problems. Knowing God had rejected him, he was immediately suspicious of anyone who became the darling of the people. The biblical author pointed out the basis for future troubles by noting, "So Saul eyed David from that day on" (18:9).

Saul's family multiplied his troubles. His own children were attracted to David. Jonathan and David entered into a covenant of brotherhood, and Michal fell in love with the youth from Bethlehem (18:1–5,20). Saul seized on this latter development to plot David's destruction. Knowing of David's and Michal's love, the king demanded a dowry of a hundred foreskins of the Philistines. Naturally, Saul believed David would be killed before he could get such a gift. Instead, David was successful, and Saul's plot failed. So the king's fear and hostility increased (18:21–29).

At this point King Saul's attempts to kill David came into the open. David was forced to flee from the king's wrath, and those who aided him faced extreme danger, if not destruction. So bitter was the king that at times he turned against his own family. Further, he even attacked and killed those of the priesthood who aided David. Despite Saul's efforts, David prospered. Saul became ever more troubled and distraught (19:1—2:23).

V. David's Actions in Saul's Last Days (1 Sam. 23:1—30:31)

Several features of David's last days under Saul's reign grab our attention. First, in spite of Saul's hostility and attempts to kill David, David refused to kill Saul even when he had the opportunity (24:1–15; 26:6–25). His mercy toward Saul was unbelievably gracious as well as politically expedient. His followers, some of whom might later have been tempted to assassinate him, saw his reverence for the "Lord's anointed." Patiently, Saul's anointed successor waited on God to raise him to the throne rather than get there by virtue of his own act of violence.

Second, Jonathan stood out in those days as an example of graciousness. As Saul's son, Jonathan was in line for the throne. For David to succeed to the throne was to disinherit Jonathan of what he could have assumed was his right. Yet Jonathan's love for David was greater than his own ambition. He encouraged his greatest rival for the throne, saying, "Fear not: for the hand of Saul my father shall not find thee; And thou shalt be king over Israel, and I shall be next unto thee; and that also Saul my father knoweth" (1 Sam. 23:17).

Third, David's relation with the Philistines in general and with Achish of Gath in particular reveal David's wisdom. What better place for him to flee from the wrath of Saul than to one of Saul's bitterest enemies? (27:1—29:11) No one would have ever thought to look for him there. Even if they had, being so deep in

Philistine territory was the best protection David could have had. In addition, David and his men almost certainly learned the process of iron smelting while they were there. This would later allow Israel to close the gap in that ancient arms race.

While fighting some of the marauders of the region, David kept the Philistines happy and delivered the people of Judah from oppression. In so doing, he cemented his southern support and honed his own skills as a general. When David at last became king of Israel, his long association with the Philistines caused them to believe that he was their protégé. This allowed him time to consolidate his kingdom before they discovered otherwise. Certainly, God's providence kept David out of any battle between the Philistines and Israel, especially the battle in which Saul and Jonathan met death.

Fourth, in the ancient Near East, soldiers were customarily paid by the booty they captured in a battle. David showed wisdom and the ability to win the allegiance of his followers when he started distributing the spoils of battle among all his soldiers, not just those who had been engaged in battle. He recognized the value to an overall military plan of those who stood guard as well as those who fought (30:1–31).

Fifth, David's humanity was clearly shown in dealing with Nabal and Abigail (25:1–44). His weakness for women began to show, a weakness ultimately revealed in his adultery with Bathsheba.

VI. David's Response to the Deaths of Saul and Jonathan (1 Sam. 31:1—2 Sam. 1:27)

The Philistines defeated Israel, bringing the deaths of Saul and his three sons, including Jonathan (1 Sam. 31:1–2). From a human standpoint, the Philistine leaders' distrust of David kept him and his troops from fighting on the Philistine side (1 Sam. 29:1–70). Fighting with Israel's enemies against Israel's army would have endangered David's political future with Israel. The voice of faith must add that the absence of Israel's future king was due to God's providence.

The wounded Saul, rather than be captured by his enemies, committed suicide. When the Philistines found the dead king and his sons, they stripped him of his armor, cut off his head, and hung his body on the walls of Beth-Shan to be the object of ridicule until the body decayed and was destroyed by the carrion eaters. Apparently, Saul's sons suffered the same fate (1 Sam. 31:3–

10,12). For the ancient Hebrews and their neighbors, every person deserved respectful burial. It was an inescapable family duty. The Philistines' act robbed the royal family of a sacred right and would have been viewed as the utmost desecration.

The men of Jabesh-Gilead heard of this act of horror. Even though all Israel had fled before the Philistines, the citizens of Jabesh-Gilead dedicated themselves to rescue the bodies of Saul and his sons. Motivation for this brave act came from one of Saul's earliest acts as king. He had rescued Jabesh-Gilead from their oppressors (1 Sam.11:1–11). Showing their allegiance to the end, they made sure the bodies of their beloved king and his sons were treated with the respect and honor due them, beyond the reach of the hostile Philistines (1 Sam. 31:11–13).

An Amalekite had apparently passed over the battlefield between the time of Saul's suicide and the time the Philistines found his body. Sensing an opportunity for personal advantage, the Amalekite stole Saul's crown and carried it to David. He reported that he had killed the wounded Saul and had brought the crown to David along with the news of his enemy's death. Apparently the Amalekite expected to be rewarded for killing Saul and for bringing the crown to David (2 Sam. 1:1–10).

David's reaction to this news again reveals his greatness. He immediately mourned the deaths of Saul and Jonathan, even though their deaths had opened the way to the throne for him. The Bible gives us no reason to doubt the future king's genuine sorrow. David's acts of mourning revealed love for Jonathan and respect for his king, Saul. Rather than reward the Amalekite, David had him executed for lifting his hand against the Lord's anointed (2 Sam. 1:11–16). Thus the young man's lies caused his own death.

David's grief so stirred him that he composed an elegy for Jonathan and Saul. The words of his grief, like all good poetry, expressed the feelings of all Israel and were treasured by them over the centuries.

> Your glory, O Israel, lies slain
> upon your high places!
> How the mighty have fallen!
> Tell it not in Gath,
> proclaim it not in the streets of
> Ashkelon;
> or the daughters of the Philistines
> will rejoice,

> the daughters of the
> uncircumcised will exult.
> (2 Sam. 1:19–20)

> Saul and Jonathan, beloved and lovely!
> In life and in death they were not divided;
>   they were swifter than eagles,
>   they were stronger than lions.
> O ye daughters of Israel, weep over Saul,
>   who clothed you with crimson, in luxury,
> who put ornaments of gold on your apparel.
>   How the mighty have fallen,
>   in the midst of the battle.
> (2 Sam. 1:23–24)

David's grief was deep and genuine. It endeared him to those who had loved and supported Saul, and it opened the way for them to transfer their love and allegiance to him as king. For the first time since Samuel had anointed him as future king, the path to the throne was open. David's patient waiting on God was about to be rewarded.

VII. David Reigns over Judah (2 Sam. 2:1—4:12)

Two events that followed the death of Saul help us understand two later features of the Hebrew monarchy. Under God's leadership David left the territory of the Philistines and went to Hebron, one of the chief cities of Judah. The people of Judah came to him and crowned him king of their tribe. At the same time, Abner, Saul's general, took Ishbosheth, one of Saul's surviving sons, and had him crowned king over the northern tribes (2:1–11).

These two events show that the people of Israel did not perceive the kingship to be wholly hereditary. To the contrary, they believed they had a voice in who was going to reign over them. This was a decided departure from other ancient Near Eastern kingdoms. The nation had two kings ruling over different tribes. This shows that the union between the southern and the northern tribes was tenuous at best. The divided monarchy that came later was probably more normal than the brief era of the united monarchy.

Again, however, David did not have all that God had promised him. He was forced to wait another seven and a half years before he ruled over the entire kingdom. Because of his faith he did this willingly. Saul's loyal followers noted David's generous treatment of the people of Jabesh-Gilead. The seeds were sown for their future support for the king from Bethlehem.

The biblical author or early scribes changed the name of Saul's son from Eshbaal (or "Ishbaal," compare 1 Chron. 8:33; 9:39) to Ishbosheth. The original name means "Man of Baal," while the later one means "Man of shame." The worship of the Canaanite Baal was always a problem for the Northern Kingdom, and the author of this change was proclaiming that it was a shame for anyone to be involved in such apostasy.

For a period of time, conflict broke out between the southern and the northern armies. This was apparently intended by the northern tribes to bring the southern region back into line. The Philistines stayed out of this conflict. They possibly assumed that David was "their" man. More likely, however, they simply assumed that any tribal warfare in Israel could only weaken the Hebrew nation for a future Philistine attack.

Two further events of this era set the final stage for David to become king over all Israel. Abner, the northern commander, entered into negotiations with David to deliver the allegiance of the northern tribes to him. In return Abner expected to remain general over the combined forces. This plan was thwarted, however, when Abner was murdered by Joab. Joab passed this act of treachery off as blood vengeance, but it more likely represented Joab's attempt to maintain his leadership of David's troops (3:12–27). About the same time Ishbosheth was murdered. His murderers brought his head to David. They apparently were expecting a reward, thinking this death removed the last obstacle to David's kingship over all the tribes of Israel north and south (4:5–8).

Once again, David's response to this act of treachery showed his greatness. He grieved over Abner and wrote a stirring elegy concerning his death. He executed Ishbosheth's murderers (3:31–35; 4:9–12). The author pointed out that "All the people took notice of it, and it pleased them; just as everything the king did pleased all the people" (3:36). By these acts, David was winning the allegiance and support of those who had followed Saul.

VIII. David's Early Reign over Israel (2 Sam. 5:1—10:19)

Following the death of Ishbosheth, the northern tribes sought out David as their king. They revealed their eagerness to have David rule by going as far south as Hebron. Once again the people revealed their belief that they had a voice in who was going to be their king (5:1–5). At long last, the promise God had made to David, the shepherd of Bethlehem, had come to pass. David was now king over all Israel. At times the reality of that promise seemed impossibly remote. At other times, it simply appeared impossible. David had waited with patient faith, and God had kept His word.

David's first problem as the king of all Israel was the location of his capitol. To rule over the land from Hebron would have put him too far from the northern tribes, possibly alienating them, since Hebron was deep in the heart of Judah. To have moved his kingdom to Saul's court or to any of the major northern cities would just as surely have alienated his southern followers, those who had supported him so long.

With a flash of genius, David chose the Jebusite city of Jerusalem as his capital. Located on the border between south and north, Jerusalem had never been occupied by the Hebrews after their entrance into the land. David attacked it, conquered it, rebuilt it, and fortified it. He turned it into his citadel (5:5–10). Having neither southern nor northern roots or traditions, it could attract all of the nation without alienating any. To this day, it is still known as "The City of David."

The Philistines finally became alarmed at David's increasing success and power. Unfortunately for them, their reaction was too late. David's victory over them marked the beginning of the end of the Philistine domination of Israel (5:17–25). During his stay among the Philistines, David's troops had apparently learned the secret of iron smelting, bringing about a balance of power in that ancient arms race.

All that remained for the final consolidation of David's authority was bringing the ark of God to Jerusalem. This act would make the city the political and religious center of the nation. When the ark was finally brought into the city, David's exuberant celebration caused a problem for Michal, his wife. She couched her rebuke in terms of jealousy (6:1–23). In all fairness we must remember that she had seen the excesses of her father Saul and remembered the end result. In any case, David was either insensitive to her problem or simply did not care. His response to her that God "chose me in place of your father" (6:21) clearly added injury to jealousy, putting an effective end to the love that they had once shared. From this point on, their marriage became one of name only, for they "had no child to the day of her death" (6:23). Tragically, David never showed the same genius or devotion in dealing with his family that he showed in ruling his people.

At this point David turned his full attention to being king over Israel. He moved from victory to victory as he faced the nation's enemies. His battles began as attempts to defend Israel against peoples who had opposed and oppressed Israel since their entrance into Canaan. The battles ended with David having enlarged the borders of his kingdom to the point of its greatest territorial expansion (8:1—10:19). After his death, Israel never again was so large and powerful. With David's successes, however, Israel's needs changed. A governmental administrator became more necessary than a military leader. New tasks and the development of new skills demanded the attention of the king.

IX. David's Personal Problems (2 Sam. 11:1—18:33)

David's change in roles from military leader to bureaucrat proved utterly frustrating to a man of action and led to the darkest period of his life. In the spring when he normally led his troops to battle, he remained behind to care for pressing government business (11:1). His heart was with his troops, but administrative burdens kept him home.

In his restless wanderings about the palace, David's eye fell on Bathsheba, and lust took over. She became pregnant. Fear of being found out made him try to cover his sin by making it appear that Bathsheba's husband, Uriah, was father of the unborn child. When that failed, David seized on his knowledge of Uriah's bravery. He gave military orders ensuring his faithful follower was killed in battle. Israel's great king had become an adulterer, a murderer, and a traitor to the loyalty of his supporters. David married Bathsheba, thinking that he had successfully covered his sins (11:1-27). He was wrong. God knew. Some of David's personal guards knew. And Nathan the prophet knew.

Prophets were an official part of a king's council in Israel, as well as throughout the ancient Near East. They were expected to speak the words of God to their king and bring him problems with which he must deal. Nathan's approach to David began as if he were doing the latter. Actually he was doing the former. His parable of the poor man's lamb aroused David's wrath, but David heard the voice of God in Nathan's words, "You are the man!" (12:7).

David could have lashed out at the prophet, even ordering his execution. To the contrary, we once again see David's greatness in his simple confession, "I have sinned" (12:13). The king's confession brought an immediate response as the prophet announced God's forgiveness. David's acts of sin and selfishness, however, bore bitter fruit the rest of his life. Even when God forgives, He does not rewrite history.

David's lust was reflected in his son Amnon's rape of his half-sister (Absalom's sister) Tamar (13:1–22). Both lust and treachery were reflected in Absalom's rebellion and in his lying with David's concubines on the roof of the palace (15:1—18:8; especially 16:22). David had pronounced a four-fold repayment on the rich man in Nathan's parable. David's murder of Uriah perhaps resulted in the king's fourfold tragedies: the death of Bathsheba's first child, Absalom's murder of Amnon, Joab's murder of Absalom, and finally in Solomon's murder of Adonijah (12:19; 13:28–29; 18:15; 1 Kings 2:23–25).

Perhaps David swallowed the bitterest fruit when his closest advisor, Ahithophel, became the moving force behind Absalom's rebellion. At first glance, Ahithophel's instigation of the rebellion makes little sense. A careful reading of the text reveals that he was the father of Eliam, who in turn was the father of Bathsheba (23:34; 11:3). Thus Absalom's rebellion was the end result of David's moments of sinful pleasure.

Little in David's life after his sin with Bathsheba and Uriah brought the king either pleasure or peace. This shows up graphically in his overwhelming grief at the death of rebellious Absalom. "O my son Absalom, my son, my son Absalom! Would I had died instead of you, O Absalom, my son, my son!" (18:33). Perhaps the major part of David's grief came because he could see the reflection of his own sin in the rebellion that brought such overwhelming sorrow.

X. David's Final Days as King (2 Sam. 19:1—24:25)

If David's time as king began with the roar of thunder, it drew to a close with a rasping wheeze. The great days of expansion and conquest seem to have given way to the sad machinations of an old man whose life had slowly decayed. One of the few flashes of his former greatness showed through in his merciful treatment of those who had lashed out at him in the days of Absalom's rebellion, as well as his generosity toward those who had supported him (19:16–39; 21:1–14).

David's final days also forced him to deal with ongoing military problems (20:1–26; 21:15–22). Occasionally, he showed flashes of his earlier military genius, but the earlier spark was gone. David had not lost his love for Yahweh nor something of his old poetic genius. While not of the same brilliance as some of his earlier poetry, his final song of faith and trust still revealed something of his old poetic genius (23:1–7). Note that the editor included a song reflecting David's earlier days (22:2–52; also found in Psalm 18 with slight modifications).

The two final events recorded in 2 Samuel are significant for quite different reasons. The first shows Israel's increasing perception of God's self-revelation. Note that 2 Samuel 24:1 says God incited David's to take a census, but 1 Chronicles 21:1 repeats the story but credits Satan with leading David to the sin (24:1; 1 Chron. 21:1). At this point in their faith pilgrimage the ancient Hebrews had no awareness of the differences between God's permissive will and His active or causative will. They simply understood that whatever happened had ultimately come from Yahweh, the sovereign Lord.

The last event was David's decision to build an altar to God in Jerusalem. When the king approached Arunah, the Jebusite offered to give the king not only the land for the altar but the animals that would be sacrificed there. David once again revealed the greatness of his love for Yahweh when he responded with the ultimate outpouring of his devotion. "I will not offer burnt offerings to the Lord my God that cost me nothing" (24:24). David showed in his own actions that devotion that costs the worshiper nothing is of little value. Solomon finally constructed the temple of Jerusalem on the site of Arunah's threshing floor.

Message

From an historical-theological perspective, the two most significant features found in 1 and 2 Samuel are the founding of the monarchy and the rise of the Hebrew prophetic movement. The latter was actually the more significant, for Israel's prophets ultimately made the more lasting contribution. Rather than waiting for people to come to them with questions, Yahweh's prophets went to their people with His message. They came to kings and to the people, expecting to be heard.

The kingship established the national identity of Israel while at the same time turning away from the direct divine authority of Yahweh. The people of Israel, as have people of many other times and places, had difficulty following a God they could not see. Immediate crises forced them to demand a visible leader to fight their battles. Out of the Hebrew kingship came Yahweh's promise to David that gave rise to their messianic hope, finally fulfilled in David's greater Son. Perhaps the ultimate message underlying both books is that Samuel voiced to Saul.

> Has the Lord as great delight in
> burnt offerings and sacrifices,
> as in obeying the voice of the Lord?
> Surely, to obey is better than sacrifice,
> and to heed than the fat of rams.
> For rebellion is no less a sin than divination,
> and stubbornness is like iniquity and idolatry.
> (1 Sam. 15:22–23)

The ultimate theme is not history, but it is faithfulness. God expects and demands faithfulness from His people.

Individual Character Studies

The three major persons who walked on this formative stage of Israel's history were Samuel, Saul, and David. All three were human, with human strengths and weaknesses. Not one of them was a plaster saint or a figure in a stained glass window. In God's providence, all had their part to play in His plan.

Samuel

The stories Hannah told Samuel about his miraculous birth had to make an impact on him. This, coupled with his training by Eli, prepared him to serve God. When his divine call is added, he was uniquely equipped to bring God's word to his people.

Samuel combined in his ministry the offices of prophet, priest, and judge. Sadly, his devotion to the service of his people brought about the neglect of his own sons, as he followed in the path of Eli, his mentor.

With the increasing pressure of the Philistines, Samuel finally granted the plea of the people for a king and anointed Saul as the first king of Israel. Samuel apparently believed the people's demand to be a rejection of his own leadership. This may have influenced his future relationship with Saul. From the standpoint of Samuel, that relationship appears to have been one of punctilious righteousness but no compassion.

He had originally sought to present Saul to the people following a dramatic casting of lots, but Saul upstaged the prophet by not being available. Later, Samuel delayed in joining Saul for the purpose of offering sacrifice before the armies of Israel went into battle. Yet as soon as Saul did it, Samuel immediately showed up, almost as if he had been waiting to see how the new king would act under pressure. Finally, when Saul disobeyed the commands of God in his attack on Amalek, Samuel publicly rebuked the king and refused to accompany him any further, an act that showed little compassion. On the other hand, Samuel genuinely seems to have grieved over Saul's failure. The king would at least have been encouraged if Samuel had let him know of his heartache. In summary, Samuel was clearly a man of God, but his humanity must never be ignored as an integral feature of his character. He died grieving over the failure of Saul and not yet seeing the fruition of David.

Saul

To Saul goes the credit of being the first king of Israel. An exceptional man physically, he seems to have been affected by an inferiority complex, a characteristic often found in people who stand out physically from their peers. Further, as Israel's first king, he had not been raised as a king's son. He naturally ascended the throne feeling unprepared for the task. This further accentuated his sense of inadequacy.

Saul seems to have longed for Samuel's approval, something he never got. He revealed himself as a man who was generous to his political opponents. In addition, he was apparently a good general. Unfortunately, he failed to understand his relationship to Yahweh. On more than one occasion he seems to have believed that he knew better than God what ought to be done.

Finally confronted with his failure by Samuel, Saul did not give up. He still continued to rule over Israel, trying to carry on. Unfortunately, he was a jealous man, spending a major portion of the latter days of his reign trying to capture and kill David, his obvious rival. In his last days, Saul seems to have suffered from some form of mental illness. To his credit, he never turned his back on his duty. In the end he died seeking to serve his people, fighting against the Philistines.

David

Like Saul, David was also unprepared for the kingship. At the same time, David was clearly the greatest king Israel ever had. His reign was always viewed as Israel's golden age. When they looked forward to an ideal future, Israel looked for a son of David who would reign over them as Messiah.

Several distinct characteristics show up in David's life as recorded in 1 and 2 Samuel. First, he was wholly devoted to God. This does not mean that he did not sin, for he was also human. In fact, a second feature of David's life appears to have been a weakness for women. Yet even in the midst of his sin, David never thought he was above the law, so he turned to God for forgiveness.

David also showed a generous nature in countless ways. His respect for Yahweh's anointed, coupled with his generosity, led the future king to deal with Saul again and again in a spirit of mercy and compassion. Further, on numerous occasions David forgave enemies, treating them with mercy. David showed himself to be courageous in the face of danger. In addition, he was a brilliant military strategist, leading his nation to the greatest territorial expansion they ever enjoyed.

Unfortunately, like Samuel and Eli before him, David failed to be the father he ought to have been. His family problems reveal his greatest failures. One of the sadder things he ever saw was the reflection of his own sin in the lives of his children. We certainly remember David for his greatness, but we dare not forget his failures. He was a man of great passion, a passion that revealed itself in his sin, in his devotion, in his compassion, in his warfare, and in his music. He won the hearts of his followers, even as he won the battles over his enemies.

Questions for Reflection and Review

1. Write one identifying sentence about the following: Uriah, Joab, Abner, Bathsheba, Amnon, Absalom, Michal, Jonathan.

2. What does the apparent use of sources by the author of 1 and 2 Samuel have to do with belief that God is the ultimate Author of Scripture?

3. Use Samuel, Saul, David, or another character of your choosing to illustrate how one does a character study of a biblical person and what one expects to learn from such a study.

4. Use the Books of 1 and 2 Samuel to discuss the relationship among sin, forgiveness, and punishment.

5. What were the political benefits of David's choice of Jerusalem as his capitol?

Bibliography

Anderson, A. A. *2 Samuel.* Vol. 11 of *Word Biblical Commentary.* Waco: Word, 1989.

Brueggemann, Walter. *First and Second Samuel.* Louisville: John Knox, 1990.

Klein, Ralph W. *1 Samuel.* Vol. 10 of *Word Biblical Commentary.* Waco: Word, 1983.

Lewis, Joe. *1 & 2 Samuel, 1 Chronicles.* Vol. 5 of *Layman's Bible Book Commentary.* Nashville: Broadman Press, 1980.

Vos, Howard F. *1, 2 Samuel: Bible Study Commentary.* Grand Rapids: Zondervan, 1983.

Chapter 6

The Books of 1 and 2 Kings

The Books of 1 and 2 Kings describe the main period of the Hebrew monarchy. Not only do they record most of what we know of the Hebrew monarchy, but they tell the story of its massive failure and final dissolution. The Books of Samuel ended in the latter part of David's reign, Israel's so-called golden age. The Books of Kings pick up the narrative with the accession of Solomon to the throne.

Although this era had its occasional times of spiritual fidelity as well as times of political and military significance, the main proclamation of these books points to a growing apostasy. This began under Solomon and proceeded until the kingdom separated into its two halves, Israel and Judah. First and 2 Kings recount the rebellion and general faithlessness of each of these two kingdoms and their rulers. Finally, the Assyrians destroyed Israel. About 722 B.C. Judah, for the same reasons, suffered the same fate under Babylon about 586/87 B.C. At that point, the Hebrew experiment with monarchy came to an end, and the narrative of 1 and 2 Kings ended.

Glossary	
The Battle of Qarqar	The **Battle of Qarqar** took place between Assyria and a number of small city-states in 853 B. C., and is important because King Ahab of Israel was there, giving us a firm date for establishing an Old Testament chronology.

Glossary	
The Black Obelisk	The **Black Obelisk** of King Shalmaneser of Assyria pictures King Jehu of Israel paying tribute in 842 B. C., giving us another firm date in Old Testament chronology and the first portrayal of a bibilical character.
Co-regency	A **co-regency** was a time when a ruling king took a son on the throne with him to share in the responsibilities of rule.
Horns of the Altar	The **horns of the altar** were projections on the four corners of the altar and were considered to be especially sacred, offering refuge or sanctuary for a person fleeing from vengeance.
Succession Narrative	The **succession narrative** is found in 2 Samuel 23:1 through 1 Kings 2:46 and describes how Solomon succeeded to the throne after David.
Syro-Ephraimitic crisis	The **Syro-Ephraimatic crisis** occurred in 735 B. C. and was that time when the kings of Syria and Israel (Ephraim) sought to force Judah into a coalitiion with them against Assyria.

Place in the Canon, Date, and Authorship

The Books of 1 and 2 Kings, like Joshua, Judges, and 1 and 2 Samuel, form part of the Hebrew canon's Former Prophets. As such they continue to use Israel's history to proclaim God's prophetic message. The authors apparently never intended 1 and 2 Kings to supply us with a full chronicle of Israel's monarchy. These books proclaim God's activities with and His messages to His people during the era of the Hebrew monarchy.

We can determine the date of the final compilation or writing of 1 and 2 Kings fairly precisely. The books end with a report of King Jehoiachin's release from prison.

> In the thirty-seventh year of the exile of King Jehoiachin of Judah, in the twelfth month, on the twenty-seventh day of the month, King Evil-merodach of Babylon, in the year that he began to reign, released King Jehoi-

achin of Judah from prison; . . . So Jehoiachin put off his prison clothes. . . .
he dined regularly in the king's presence. (2 Kings 25:27,29)

Four things from this statement demand our attention. (1)
Evil-Merodach, known in Babylonian records as Amel-Marduk, began to reign about 562 B.C., and the author knew of this; therefore,
2 Kings could not have been completed earlier than this. (2) The
author knew that for some time after his release Jehoiachin dined
at the king's table and that at the time of the writing of this book
he was no longer living. This means that 2 Kings was not finished
until some time after his release in 562 B.C. (3) In addition, the
end of Israel's Babylonian exile in 539 B.C. is not mentioned in 2
Kings. Although this is an argument from silence, it is inconceiv-
able that such an important event in Hebrew history was not mentioned if the author knew about it. (4) Finally, Neriglissar
succeeded Evil-Merodach on the throne of Babylon about 560 B.C.
Since neither he nor his successor, Nabonidus, are mentioned in
connection with Jehoiachin, it is most likely that the book was finished before Evil-Merodach's reign ended.

Thus I conclude that the Books of Kings were completed between 562 and 539 B.C. Most likely, the task was completed shortly
before Neriglissar ascended the throne of Babylon in 560 B.C. If it
were later than this, the author made no reference to subsequent
events.

The division between 1 and 2 Kings appears to be quite artificial. First Kings ends with the beginning of the reign of Ahaziah
of Israel, while 2 Kings begins with the end of that reign (1 Kings
22:51; 2 Kings 1:2–18). Similarly, 2 Samuel ends with the last words
of David, and 1 Kings begins with David's final days (2 Sam 23:1; 1
Kings 1:1—2:12). We noted in the preceding chapter the artificial
division between 1 and 2 Samuel. In the Septuagint the four books
are designated as 1, 2, 3, and 4 Kingdoms. Apparently, they were
originally one book that was divided into four volumes simply to
make them easier to handle.

We have already noted that these four books, along with
Joshua and Judges, were originally written or compiled by people
who evaluated history by the standards of Deuteronomy. None of
these books shows the influence of Deuteronomy as fully as 1 and
2 Kings. Suggesting that these were written or edited by the Deuteronomic historian(s) is as close as we can come to identifying an
author. We do know that the author used several sources. Three
of these are specifically identified: "the book of the acts of So-

lomon"(1 Kings 11:41, NASB) "the Book of the Chronicles of the Kings of Judah" (1 Kings 14:29, NASB) and "the Book of the Chronicles of the Kings of Israel" (1 Kings 14:19, NASB). All of these appear to have been the official court records of the various kings. Lest there be any confusion, the latter two are in no way to be identified with the biblical Books of 1 and 2 Chronicles.

Scholars have also suggested that three other sources were probably used. The first of these is frequently called "the succession narrative" and is usually identified as 2 Samuel 23:1 through 1 Kings 2:46.[1] This tells the arrangements for Solomon to succeed David on the throne. Such a historical source may have been a part of David's official records or a part of Nathan's or Gad's chronicles from that time. The author of Chronicles used these last two, so they were certainly available in the time of the writing of 1 Kings (compare 1 Chron. 29:29–30). Since this material appears to be a literary unit, there is the possibility that this source existed, although many scholars deny it.

Scholars often suggest a second source preserved in 1 Kings 20:1–43 and 22:1–40. These two chapters evaluate Ahab's reign in a more favorable light than the other parts of the story. While this may be true, we must acknowledge that Ahab may have had both good and bad points. This may have been a separate source but appears much less likely to have been so.

A third source is often suggested as containing the stories of the prophets, primarily seen in the material related to Elijah, Elisha, and Isaiah. A superficial reading shows that the Elijah/Elisha materials are different from that which surrounds them.

The biographical material on Isaiah (2 Kings 18:13—20:19) is almost identical to that found in Isaiah 36:1—39:8. This material was possibly put together by prophetic disciples and collected in a scroll of prophets' biographies. The author of Kings then drew on these biographies as these books were put into their final form.

Organization

The Books of Kings covers Hebrew history from the last days of David (about 961 B.C.) to Jehoiachin's release from prison (about 561 B.C.). Obviously, the author was quite selective with his material. The choice of subjects to be included apparently was

---

1. See "Succession Narrative," *Mercer Dictionary of the Bible* (Mercer University Press, 1990), 859.

made on theological rather than historical grounds. The author's intent seems to have been to tell what God was doing through the selected events. Events seem to have been recorded primarily to give the background for the faith proclaimed through them. This does not mean the information given is unimportant.

Forms for Introducing and Concluding Reigns.—The structure of 1 and 2 Kings is more distinct and highly organized than any book of the Bible. A standard form for the introduction and the conclusion or evaluation is used for the reigns of each of the kings. The framework for the kings of Judah usually follows this pattern.

Introduction: "In the _____ year of _____ king of Israel, began _____ the son of _____ the king of Judah to reign. He was _____ years old when he began to reign and he reigned _____ years in Jerusalem. And his mother's name was _____ from _____." (The precise wording of this formula occasionally varies. Some apparent variations in English translations are frequently due to translators.)

Significant Details of the Reign.—The author selected facts that furthered his prophetic purposes.

Conclusion: "And the rest of his acts, and all that he did, are they not written in the Book of the Chronicles of the Kings of Judah? So he slept with his fathers, and they buried him with his fathers in the city of David, and _____ his son reigned in his stead."

The formula for the kings of Israel varies from the one used for the kings of Judah. We expect the source reference to also vary since it is from the "Book of the Chronicles of the Kings of Israel." The king's mother is not identified, nor is the king's age on accession given for the kings of Israel.

In both formulas the reign of each king is judged or evaluated. Only Hezekiah and Josiah of Judah are praised unconditionally. No other king of Judah received such praise. Except for these two kings all were rebuked for their idolatry. Any praise for faithfulness was limited by the information that they did not abolish the "high places." In addition, the kings of Israel are consistently evaluated either as having walked in or failed to depart from the sins of "Jeroboam the son of Nebat." In the few instances when this distinctive formulaic approach to the king's reign is not used precisely, the reason for its omission is usually obvious.

Patterns for Shifting Between Israel and Judah.—The author followed a strange pattern in dealing with the reigns of kings of Israel and Judah who were contemporaries. The author regularly interrupted the narrative of the reign of one king at the point a new king ascended the throne of the other kingdom. He related the details of the reign of the new king before returning to his original subject. Events occurring after the death of the king originally being considered were often told before the author returned to the king's reign to tell of his death. Frequently this system confuses the unsuspecting reader unfamiliar with the system.

The Problem of Absolute Chronology.—Few concerns of Old Testament studies have been as complex and difficult as the attempt to understand the chronological data found in Kings. To deal with the history of Israel and Judah as reported in Kings and to place it against the appropriate background of ancient Near Eastern history, we need an absolute chronology. This cannot be determined by an investigation of the biblical text because the biblical writers do not give us sufficient information to develop a chronology. The chronology of Assyria, however, can be established with extraordinary precision.

Assyrian annals record an eclipse of the sun that modern astronomers can date to 763 B.C. Based on that absolute date and calculating backwards, the date of the Battle of Qarqar can be established as 853 B.C. That is important because, according to the Assyrian records, King Ahab of Israel fought against Assyria at that battle. This gives us an absolute date in the period of the Hebrew monarchy.

The black obelisk of King Shalmaneser III shows King Jehu of Israel paying tribute to the Assyrian king in 842 B.C., giving us a second absolute date. Using these two dates as a starting point and calculating forward and backward, we arrive at other dates in that era.[2]

The Problem of Relative Chronology.—The Books of Kings provide us so much data that the task of using it all becomes quite chaotic. Each biblical event must be aligned before or after all other dates. Such an alignment sets all events in relation to one another, thus providing a relative chronology. Scholars seek to assign absolute dates to each event. Although the issue is far too complex to

---

2. For more detail on the nature of the problem, see Robert L. Cate, *These Sought a Country* (Nashville: Broadman Press, 1985), 33 ff.; Edwin R. Thiele, *The Mysterious Numbers of the Hebrew Kings*, 3rd ed. (Grand Rapids: Zondervan, 1983); W. H. Barnes, *Studies in the Chronology of the Divided Monarchy of Israel*, Harvard Semitic Monographs 48 (Atlanta: Scholars Press, 1991); John Hayes and Paul Hooker, *A New Chronology for the Kings of Israel and Judah* (Atlanta: John Knox, 1988).

be discussed in detail, the following may serve to illustrate the problem.

The kingdom divided following Solomon's death, with Rehoboam becoming king of Judah and Jeroboam becoming king of Israel. We will call that year "0." From that time in Judah, Rehoboam reigned seventeen years, Abijam three years, and Asa forty-one years (1 Kings 14:21; 15:2,10). At the same time in Israel, Jeroboam reigned twenty-two years, Nadab two years, Baasha twenty-four years, Elah two years, Zimri seven days, Omri twelve years, and Ahab came to the throne in the thirty–eighth year of Asa king of Judah (1 Kings 14:20; 15:25,33; 16:8,15,23,29). When Ahab came to the throne, sixty-two years (22 + 2 + 24 + 2 + 0 [7 days] + 12) had passed in Israel. Yet in Judah only fifty-eight years (17 + 3 + 38) had passed. Immediately, a major problem becomes apparent. If these kinds of calculations are carried further, the problem only gets worse. More information about dating systems or a scholarly theory to explain the date is needed.

Some interpreters have proposed that the biblical statements relating the events of one kingdom to those of the other kingdom were added to the original biblical material at a much later date and should be ignored. Others have been selective with biblical data, usually preferring data relating to one kingdom over the other. Ultimately these scholars want to make the data fit into other ancient Near Eastern chronologies. Finally, some have simply ignored all the biblical chronological data. Remarkably, the results of these various reconstructions do not vary much from one another. Each of the approaches assumes that the ancient Hebrew authors could not do simple addition.

Edwin R. Thiele made a radically new approach to the problem in the middle of this century.[3] Thiele began with the assumption that these ancient historians were not nincompoops. He assumed that the basic problem was not one of having essentially inaccurate data, but it was with modern historians having a faulty understanding of the data.

Thiele began by studying the variety of methods other ancient Near Eastern nations used in recording their chronologies. Some nations began their year in the fall. Others used the spring, thus causing years to have inconsistent beginning times. Further, some counted the years of a king's reign from the time of the New

---

3. Thiele, *The Mysterious Numbers.*

Year celebration following his accession, while others counted it from the time of actual accession. Since they seldom used fractions of years, counting from the time of actual accession meant that the last year of one king's reign and the first year of his successor were counted as the same year. Each transition immediately added one year to the over-all total. An aging or sick king frequently had his son serve with him as a co-regent. Unfortunately, however, both father and son got credit for the years when both kings served, further enlarging the total for the nation.

Building on this, Thiele reconstructed the chronology of Israel and Judah. He assumed that when either of these kingdoms were under Assyrian domination, they were forced to use the Assyrian method of reckoning. When they threw off the Assyrian yoke, they expressed their independence by shifting to a different system. A detailed analysis of the text convinced Thiele of some co-regencies in addition to those the biblical text specifically identified. Thiele's approach has shown the biblical data to be understandable. The problem was our ignorance, not the authors' inaccuracies.

Content Outline

The division of David's kingdom into Judah and Israel and the fall of the Northern Kingdom provide the major content structure for the Books of Kings. We will follow the text from the beginning to the end, and we will not identify the particular book in our citations except where it overlaps in an outline section.

Part One: The End of the United Monarchy (1:1—11:43)

   I. David's final days (1:1—2:11)

      A. The struggle for succession (1:1–53)

      B. David's death (2:1–11)

  II. Solomon's reign (2:12—11:43)

      A. Solomon's consolidation of power (2:12–46)

      B. Solomon's wisdom and wealth (3:1—4:34)

      C. The building of the temple (5:1—9:9)

      D. Solomon in all his glory (9:10—10:29)

      E. Solomon's failures (11:1–43)

Part Two: The Divided Monarchy, Israel and Judah Together (1 Kings 12:1—2 Kings 17:41)

  I. Division and conflict (12:1—16:20)

      A. The time of division (12:1–33)

      B. Prophetic confrontation of Jeroboam (13:1—14:20)

      C. Rehoboam, Abijam, and Asa of Judah (14:21—15:24)

      D. Intrigue and assassination in Israel (15:25—16:20)

  II. The era of Israelite supremacy (1 Kings 16:21—2 Kings 8:29)

      A. Omri and Ahab of Israel (16:21—22:40)

          1. Political developments (16:21–34)

          2. Confrontations with Elijah (17:1—19:21)

          3. Ahab's Syrian wars (20:1–34)

          4. Death sentence on Ahab (20:35–43)

          5. Ahab's greed with Naboth and his repentance (21:1–29)

          6. Micaiah and the death of Ahab (22:1–40)

      B. Jehoshaphat of Judah and Ahaziah of Israel (1 Kings 22:41—2 Kings 2:25)

      C. Elisha, Jehoram of Israel, and Joram of Judah (3:1—8:29)

  III. The prophetic revolution (9:1—14:20)

      A. Jehu's revolt (9:1—10:36)

      B. The Athaliah crisis in Judah (11:1—12:21)

      C. Political developments and Elisha's death (13:1—14:20)

  IV. Israelite revival and collapse (14:21—17:41)

      A. Apparent revitalization of Israel (14:21—15:15)

      B. The ultimate collapse of Israel (15:16—17:41)

Part Three: The Divided Monarchy, Judah Alone (18:1—25:30)

  I. Hezekiah's accomplishments and failures (18:1—20:21)

      A. Accomplishments (18:1–12)

      B. Confrontation with Sennacherib (18:13—19:37)

      C. Hezekiah's sickness and death (20:1–21)

II.　Apostasy and reform (21:1—23:30)
　　A.　The evil of Manasseh and Amon (21:1–26)
　　B.　Josiah's reform (22:1—23:30)
III.　The last days of Judah (23:31—25:30)
　　A.　Rebellion (23:31—24:17)
　　B.　Zedekiah's weakness (24:18—25:7)
　　C.　Babylonian exile (25:8–30)

Historical Table

The following historical table of the Hebrew kings will help you follow the biblical narrative.[4] The dates of Samuel, Saul, David, and Solomon represent only approximate dates. The others are established according to Theile's system.

UNITED MONARCHY		
1100 B.C.	Samuel, 1050–1020	
	Saul, 1020–1000	
1000 B.C.	David, 1000–961	
	Solomon, 961–931	
DIVIDED MONARCHY		
	Israel	**Judah**
1000 B.C.	Jeroboam I, 931–910	Rehoboam, 931–913
	Abijam, 913–911	
	*Nadab, 910–909	Asa, 911–870

---

4. This is taken with some slight omissions and modifications from Cate, *These Sought a Country*, 399–401.

DIVIDED MONARCHY		
900 B.C.	Baasha, 909–886	
	*Elah, 886–885	
	*Zimri, 885 (7 days)	
	Omri, 885–874	
	Ahab, 874–853	Jehoshaphat, (873) 870–848
	Ahaziah, 853–852	
	*Jehoram, 852–841	Jehoram, (853) 848–841
		*Ahaziah, 841
	Jehu, 841–814	*Athaliah, 841–835
		*Joash, 835–796
	Jehoahaz, 814–798	
800 B.C.	Joash, 798–782	*Amaziah, 796–767
	Jeroboam II, (793) 782–753	Azariah (Uzziah), (791) 767–74
	*Zechariah, 753–752	
	*Shallum, 752	
	Menahem, 752–742	
	*Pekahiah, 742–740	
	*Pekah, (752) 740–732	Jotham, (750) 740–732
	*Hoshea, 732–722	Ahaz, (735) 732–716
	[Fall of Samaria, 722/21]	

DIVIDED MONARCHY		
700 B.C.		Hezekiah, 715–687
		Manasseh, (696) 687–642
		Amon, 642–640
		Josiah, 640–609
		Jehoahaz, 609
600 B.C.		Jehoiakim, 609–598
		Jehoiachin, 598–597
		Zedekiah, 597–586
		[Fall of Jerusalem, 586]

NOTE: Dates given in parentheses are when a co-regency began. Kings marked with an asterisk (*) were assassinated; however, Zimri actually committed suicide to escape assassination.

The political instability of the Northern Kingdom is quite noticeable. Eight kings were assassinated with an accompanying change of dynasty in a span of less than two centuries. The ninth and final assassination (execution) brought on the end of their kingdom. Judah, on the other hand, was relatively stable for their entire history with the exception of the last half of the ninth century (850–800). At that time the nation endured four assassinations. With the exception of the brief reign of Athaliah there was no change of dynasty. The house of David always ruled over the Southern Kingdom. This gave them a political stability that their northern relatives never enjoyed.

Summary of Contents

The high point of David's reign in 2 Samuel was also the high point of Israel's monarchy. Beginning with David's decline and continuing throughout 1 and 2 Kings, Israel's kingdom never again reached the level of significance of those early glory days. The narrative of Kings picks up where 2 Samuel left off, in the last days of David.

Part One.
The End of the United Monarchy
(1:1—11:43)

Judges ended and 1 Samuel began with the Hebrew people longing for a king (Judg. 18:1; 19:1; 21:25; 1 Sam. 8:4–5,19–20). God granted their request, but Saul did not fulfill their hopes for military victory and national greatness. Such hopes came to full fruition with David. The costs of a strong national government and an effective administration proved to be higher than the people of Israel were willing to pay. Coupled with the human weaknesses and the political scheming of their kings, these costs led the people to withdraw support from their government even as God began to withdraw His power from their kings. The first hints of the problem come to our attention in David's last days.

I. David's Final Days (1:1—2:11)

Two main features characterize the end of David's reign as king of Israel, one personal and the other political. The personal development came during David's final illness when his counselors sought to determine how sick he was. Their crude method was to put an attractive young girl from Shunem in bed with him. When her presence failed to arouse him, they knew he was on the verge of death (1:1–4). Sadly, their method reveals his widespread sexual reputation.

The political development of David's final days centered around the issue of succession: who would follow David on Israel's throne? This may seem strange to people used to European history. There the oldest living son was always expected to succeed. In Israel this was not so. First, the people had a voice in who their new king would be. Further, David's advisors expected that the king's popularity with the people was such that anyone whom he named as successor would be acclaimed by the people. They were right.

The two contenders for the throne were Adonijah, David's son by Haggith, and Solomon, David's son by Bathsheba. Each had support from members of David's court, probably in the anticipation of their own advancement if their candidate was successful. Adonijah found support from Joab, the commander of David's army, and Abiathar, one of the king's priests. Behind Solomon stood Nathan the prophet and Zadok, another of David's priests. Their intrigue and Nathan's effective planning caused David to declare Solomon as his successor. David ordered Nathan and Zadok to arrange for the people to acclaim Solomon as their king (1:5–48).

When Adonijah became aware that Solomon had been named king, he feared for his life. To escape Solomon's expected vengeance, Adonijah fled to the horns of the altar (1:50). The "horns" were projections on the corners of the altar. Blood from sacrificed animals was applied to them in Hebrew rituals, thus making them especially sacred (Ex. 27:2). Holding on to them offered special protection and a place of refuge for those seeking to escape the vengeance of their enemies. Solomon assured Adonijah that he should not fear and that there would be peace between them if Adonijah would be loyal to the new king (1:49–53).

David's last words to Solomon revealed greatness and pettiness. He charged Solomon to be faithful and obedient to God and to be merciful to those who had befriended the king in his hour of need. The old king's bitterness showed through in his words to Solomon to exact vengeance on Joab and Shimei (2:1–9). One may find it hard to believe that those bitter words came from one who throughout his life had showed both his awareness of God's mercy to him and his ability to be merciful to others. Following that admonition, David died (2:10–11).

Tragically, David's last words portray an angry, bitter man, not a great one. The Bible does not hide the weaknesses and failures of its heroes, reminding us once again that the story focuses not on David's greatness but on God's.

II. Solomon's Reign (2:12–11:43)

Immediately following David's death, Solomon began to consolidate his kingdom in the manner of a typical oriental despot. Anyone or anything that might threaten his reign was eliminated. The process was stimulated by Adonijah's request for Abishag, David's concubine (2:12–22). In the ancient Near East, whoever possessed the king's harem had a claim on the throne. Realizing that the mere existence of an older brother would always be a threat to his power, Solomon had him executed (2:23–25). Following that, King Solomon acted swiftly to eliminate other real or potential threats to his power. He apparently feared to execute a priest of Yahweh, so he banished Abiathar from Jerusalem because of his support of Adonijah (2:26–27). He had no such qualms when it came to Joab, however. In carrying out the request of his late father and executing Joab, Solomon violated the sanctuary offered by the horns of the altar (1 Sam. 2:28–34). He further tried to deal with Shimei (compare 2 Sam. 16; 19) by placing him under house arrest. When Shimei violated the terms of their agreement, he was executed (1 Kings 2:36–46).

Thus "the kingdom was established in the hand of Solomon" (1 Kings 2:46).

Unlike his father, who had waited patiently for God to give him the kingdom, Solomon swiftly seized the power. This reflected an attitude of high-handed self-indulgence, an attitude that became characteristic of Solomon's reign.

Early days of Solomon's reign reveal the many sides of his character. They also showed the nature of David's kingdom. The customary way of sealing treaties between rulers in the ancient Near East was for the king of least importance to give a daughter to the other king or to his son. The pharaoh of Egypt demonstrated the respect Israel held among the nations when he gave his daughter to Solomon.

Yahweh gave Solomon the opportunity to ask for anything his heart desired. Instead of asking for wealth or power, Solomon showed the greatness of his spirit by asking for wisdom to govern his people (3:6–9). The king used that wisdom as he governed the people, but he may have failed to use it in his own family.

Solomon gained a reputation throughout his kingdom for both his wealth and his wisdom (4:20–34). His early days also revealed an initial ability as an administrator as he gathered a council of advisors around him and appointed deputies over the administrative districts he had made in the land (4:1–19). Recognizing the threat that the old tribal consciousness of the Hebrews had caused David, Solomon apparently was seeking to divide his land into regions that crossed over the old tribal boundaries. However, a potential problem glimmered on the king's horizon. The cost of his government was becoming exorbitant. Tax income met the immediate costs, but the ultimate cost was the division of the kingdom.

Solomon is most remembered in the Old Testament for his building of the temple in Jerusalem (5:1—9:9). While not his most significant act from either a political or an economic standpoint, from the perspective of Israel's covenant relation with Yahweh, this was his most memorable accomplishment.

Numerous artists and model builders have sought to depict the temple. They base their depictions on the relatively sparse biblical data and on what we know of similar buildings from that region of the world and from that period of ancient history. No such models can be precisely accurate. Obviously, the temple was beautiful and impressive from an architectural standpoint.[5]

Perhaps the most important feature of the temple was that it was finally built. Israel at last had a national shrine and center for worship. That symbolized their transition from being nomads or wandering slaves to being a kingdom among kingdoms. The narrative makes it clear that extravagance marked both the building and the dedication of the temple. Such extravagance was motivated by an extravagant dedication to a God who had dealt extravagantly with His people. For the rest of Israel's history, the temple symbolized to the people of Israel the presence of Yahweh in their midst. Sadly, they ultimately became so self-assured in this that they almost seem to have worshiped the temple of the Lord instead of the Lord of the temple. (Compare Jer. 7:1–15; 26:1–15.)

Measured only by his economic accomplishments, Solomon was the greatest of any of the Hebrew kings (9:10—10:29). Solomon extended Israel's economic power by venturing into international commerce. His ventures brought great wealth to the nation. Internally, Solomon built major fortresses all over the land. Unfortunately for both Israel and Solomon, his accomplishments also sowed the seeds that ultimately sprouted into the downfall of his kingdom. To achieve all that he did, Solomon had to have a great deal of labor. This led him to draft the fiercely independent Hebrews into forced labor battalions. Ultimately that led to such unrest among them that the tenuous union of the kingdom disintegrated after his death.

In addition to arousing the unrest and displeasure of his people, Solomon's actions also aroused the displeasure of God. Solomon had filled his harem with wives attained as seals to foreign treaties. To please these foreign wives, Solomon built shrines to their gods and began to participate in their worship (11:1–9). His self-assurance led him to consolidate his authority through trampling the sensitivities of his people. He lost his kingdom through trampling on his covenant with Yahweh.

Note the part that a prophet played in the end of Solomon's kingdom. The prophets of God, beginning with Samuel and

---

5. A fascinating article on the temple accompanied by beautiful pictures of probably the best modern reconstruction of it can be found in "Herod's Temple in East Anglia," *Biblical Archaeology Review*, vol. 19, no. 5, 62–67.

Nathan, clearly felt that they had an authority in the kingdom. Ahijah, seeing Solomon's apostasy, used a symbolic act to announce that Yahweh had given the northern tribes to Jeroboam, one of Solomon's labor leaders. For all of his mighty accomplishments, Solomon died as a failure, rejected by his people and his God.

Part Two.
The Divided Monarchy, Israel and Judah Together
(1 Kings 12:1—2 Kings 17:41)

Apparently, Israel's tribal union never represented a strong national commitment. To the contrary, in the time of the united monarchy outside pressures drove the tribes together in search of a king. Allegiance to David, the strong charismatic leader, tied the tribes together. Solomon's excesses, however, brought the common political commitment of the various tribes to an end. Since Solomon's heritage was of the south, the northern tribes had had enough.

I. Division and Conflict (12:1—16:20)

After Solomon's death the leaders of the tribes gathered at Shechem to anoint a new king (12:1–16). The choice of a location other than Jerusalem for this convocation shows the presence of suspicion if not of open hostility on the part of the northern tribes. The northern tribes asked Rehoboam, Solomon's son, to relax some of Solomon's harsh policies. Rehoboam offered even harsher treatment. At that point, the kingdom did not divide; it shattered, never to be reunited.

The northern tribes selected Jeroboam, the fugitive leader from Solomon's labor battalions, as their king (12:17–24). As an exile, Jeroboam had found refuge in Egypt. That nation apparently supported his rise to the kingship of the northern tribes. Egypt's policy was to create as much trouble as possible for their Jewish neighbors, believing that anything that troubled or weakened them was to Egypt's benefit.

During the early years of separation, the Northern Kingdom with larger territory and population was able to dominate the Southern Kingdom. Also, the Northern Kingdom controlled all four major north-south highways in Palestine, while the Southern

Kingdom only set astride one. With this economic advantage the Northern Kingdom was also generally more prosperous.

The Northern Kingdom was known as Israel, but also was called Ephraim, since that was their largest tribe. The Southern Kingdom was usually known as Judah, as that was their dominant tribe. Following the final collapse of the Northern Kingdom, the names Israel and Judah seem to have been used interchangeably for the Southern Kingdom.

Jeroboam's first task as Israel's king was to make sure that nothing led the northern peoples back to the house of David. His greatest fear was the lure of the Jerusalem temple. Following the establishment of his capital at Shechem, he built or refurbished shrines at Dan and Bethel near the northern and southern borders of his kingdom. At those shrines he set up golden calves for the people of Israel to worship. His purpose for doing that may have differed from what we assume. Canaanite drawings show Baal standing on a calf. Jeroboam may have been representing the invisible Yahweh on the back of the calves he had set up. In any case the people clearly worshiped the calves, and thus Jeroboam had led Israel to sin (12:25–33).

Such sin meant the prophets once again became involved in governmental affairs. They confronted and condemned the king's acts.   Ultimate judgment was passed on him and his kingdom (13:1—14:20). Still political powers tolerated such prophetic confrontation. This reveals the foundation of the Hebrew kingdom(s) was thoroughly religious.

During the early years of the division patterns were established that became characteristic of both kingdoms. In the south, Rehoboam was succeeded on the throne of Judah by his son Abijam who was in turn succeeded by his son Asa (14:21—15:24). All of them were involved in some form of idolatry, although Asa at least carried out a minor religious reform. In spite of this, however, Judah exhibited political stability.

Israel showed no stability. Of her first five kings, two were assassinated, and a third committed suicide to escape being assassinated. In addition, her rulers continued to carry out the idolatrous policies of Jeroboam (15:25—16:20). While David's example of reverence toward the anointed king influenced his own family, it never had any impact in the north.

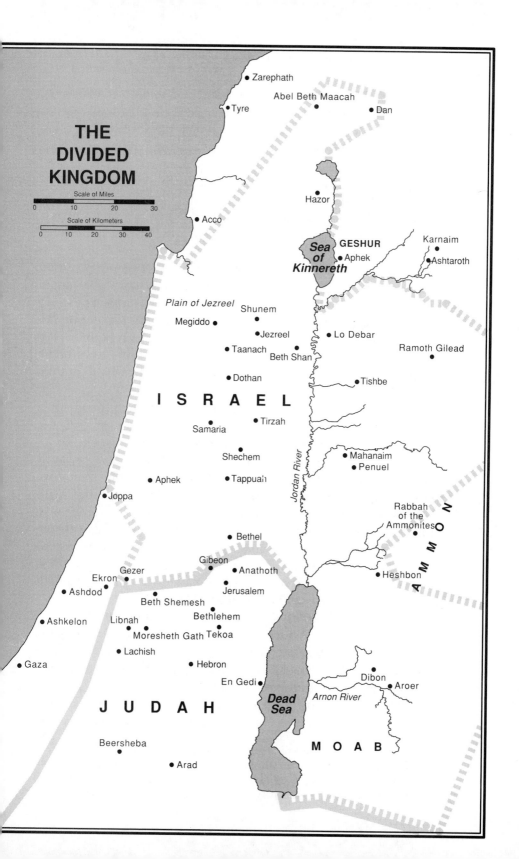

THE DIVIDED KINGDOM

Scale of Miles
0   10   20   30

Scale of Kilometers
0   10   20   30   40

Zarephath
Abel Beth Maacah
Tyre
Dan
Acco
Hazor
Sea of Kinnereth
GESHUR
Aphek
Karnaim
Ashtaroth
Plain of Jezreel
Shunem
Megiddo
Jezreel
Lo Debar
Ramoth Gilead
Taanach
Beth Shan
Dothan
Tishbe
I S R A E L
Tirzah
Samaria
Jordan River
Shechem
Mahanaim
Penuel
Aphek
Tappuah
Joppa
Rabbah of the Ammonites
Bethel
A M M O N
Gibeon
Gezer
Anathoth
Heshbon
Ekron
Ashdod
Jerusalem
Beth Shemesh
Ashkelon
Libnah
Bethlehem
Moresheth Gath
Tekoa
Lachish
Gaza
Hebron
Dibon
Aroer
En Gedi
Arnon River
Dead Sea
J U D A H
M O A B
Beersheba
Arad

II.   The Era of Israelite Supremacy (1 Kings 16:21—2 Kings 8:29)

For their first fifty years the two Hebrew kingdoms had to deal with each other and with the nations that surrounded them while searching for their own identity. At the end of that era, Israel was involved in a civil war. Omri controlled part of the nation, and Tibni controlled the other part. In a masterful understatement of that struggle, the biblical author described its culmination with the words: "But the people who followed Omri overcame the people who followed Tibni . . . so Tibni died, and Omri became king" (16:22).

Omri's accession to the throne of Israel initiated an era when the Northern Kingdom seems almost totally to have dominated their southern brothers (16:21–28). In fact, Judah appears to have been little more than an Israelite vassal throughout this period. Although the entire reign of Omri is described in only eight verses, he was such a significant ruler that from that time onward the mighty Assyrians regularly referred to Israel as "The Land of Omri."

Omri was followed on the throne of Israel by his son Ahab (16:29–34). From the perspective of the biblical narrative, the most significant feature of Ahab's reign was his marriage to Jezebel, daughter of the king of Sidon. This was almost certainly done to confirm a treaty between the two kings, with Ahab obviously being considered the more influential of the two kings. With the new wife came new gods. Jezebel imported into Israel the worship of the Baal of Phoenicia. Such worship brought false prophets and idolatrous practices. (Note that while the Canaanite gods were called Baals and the Phoenician god was called Baal, these are not the same. To the contrary, the Phoenician Baal was a high god while the Canaanite Baals were local gods.)

Another indication of the importance and power of Ahab of Israel is found in the Assyrian records from that era.[6] At the Battle of Qarqar in 853 B.C. the Assyrians faced a coalition of smaller kingdoms. Ahab of Israel brought a far larger contingent of chariots than any other nation involved.

What really made the period important, however, was not the power of the Hebrew kings but the prophets of Yahweh. What the

---

6. At least from the time of Ahab almost to the end of the Hebrew monarchy, the Assyrians played a major role in the history of the Hebrew kingdoms. A good survey of them as a nation is found in Saggs' "The Assyrians," *Peoples of Old Testament Times* (Clarendon Press, 1973), 156–78

kings were doing was not nearly as important as what God was doing. Elijah first appeared with the announcement of a drought and famine Yahweh was sending as judgment on Israel's idolatry (17:1—18:46). This period was concluded with the great contest between Elijah and the prophets of Baal. Following his victory, Elijah's humanity was revealed when he fled for his life at the threat of Jezebel. The exhausted prophet was refreshed and encouraged by Yahweh and sent back to his task (19:1–21).

Elijah's final confrontation with Ahab took place over the king's desire for the vineyard of Naboth (20:35—21:29). Two things Jezebel never understood: (1) Hebrew kings felt constrained to obey the law, and (2) prophets of God had an authority over the king. The final confrontation brought the prophet's announcement that the kingdom would not stand in Ahab's line.

From a political standpoint, his wars with Syria and their allies (20:1–34; 22:1–40) characterized Ahab's reign. Apparently, Jehoshaphat of Judah (22:41–50) accompanied Ahab during those campaigns. Israel was victorious, but Ahab lost his life. Ahaziah succeeded to the throne of Israel and immediately faced a war with rebellious Moab (1:1–18). Following in the idolatrous path of his parents, he turned to the worship of Baal-zebub. Once again, Elijah intervened with a message of judgment on his king.

Elijah's mysterious journey into the heavens (2 Kings 2:1–14) did not leave Israel prophetless. His disciple Elisha filled his shoes (2:1–25). In many ways Elisha's ministry remarkably paralleled that of his master. He was involved with ordinary human problems as well as with the affairs of nations, particularly in the on-going Syrian wars (3:13—8:15). As this period drew to a close, Israel and Judah had a king named Jehoram (3:1–12; 8:16–23). (Joram is a contraction of Jehoram.) When Jehoram of Judah died, his son Ahaziah, who had the same name as the father of Jehoram of Israel, succeeded him (8:24–29). These identical names afford a basis for confusion among those who are not careful with details in their study of this period.

III. The Prophetic Revolution (9:1—14:20)

The apostasy and sinful rebellion that Jezebel had brought with her to Israel spread to Judah. When Jehoram became king of Judah, he married Athaliah, the daughter of Ahab and Jezebel (8:18,24; 11:1). Athaliah brought her mother's influence toward apostasy to Judah. Thus the Southern Kingdom walked down the same path on which her mother had led Israel. At this point, the prophets of Yahweh intervened.

Jehu led the military revolt against the Phoenician apostasy in Israel, but God's prophets inspired and motivated it. Thus Bible students usually refer to "the prophetic revolution" (9:1—10:36). While leading Israel's attack on Ramoth-Gilead, Jehu met a disciple of Elisha, who anointed him king. He immediately set forth, assassinating both Jehoram (Joram) of Israel and Ahaziah of Judah (9:24,27). Next, he led the brutal assassination of Jezebel and the slaughter of all the worshipers of the Phoenician Baal in Israel. While Jehu's goals of purging and purification were praiseworthy, his methods of carrying them out were excessive. Almost a century later the prophet Hosea called the nation to judgment because of it (Hos. 1:4–5).

This period witnessed an event unique in Judah's history. A woman, Athaliah, Jezebel's daughter (11:1—12:21), seized the throne. Following her son's death, Athaliah called for the execution of anyone who might have a legitimate claim to the throne. The horror increases when we realize that these would have been her grandchildren. Athaliah's reign was the only time in Judah's history when a person outside the line of David sat on the throne of Judah. Her own daughter, Jehosheba, however, foiled her plans. Jehoseba took the infant Joash and hid him in the chambers of Jehoiada the priest.

When Joash was seven years old, he was acclaimed king of Judah. Immediately, Athaliah was executed. Abandoning the apostasy of his grandmother, Joash sponsored a major refurbishing of the temple. Delays could not prevent this from becoming the great accomplishment of his reign.

Near the end of this period confusion again faces us: the northern and the southern king bore the same name, Jehoash (Joash). The ongoing conflict with Syria still held the military and political attention of both of the Hebrew kingdoms. The death of Elisha brought the prophetic revolution to an end (13:1—14:20). King Jehoash of Israel showed Elisha's importance, calling the dying prophet "The chariots of Israel and its horsemen!" (13:14). The prophet of Yahweh was the real strength of his nation, not their army.

IV.   Israelite Revival and Collapse (14:21—17:41)

Shortly after 800 B.C., Jeroboam came to the throne of Israel, and Azariah (Uzziah) began a co-regency in Judah (14:21—15:7). The times offered great opportunities to both kingdoms. The Syrians and Assyrians to the north and Egypt to the south were all experiencing internal difficulties. Thus they offered no significant threat to the Hebrew kingdoms for over fifty years.

Amos and Hosea in the north and Isaiah in the south give us the best understanding of this era. For the first time since David, reduced international threats offered Israel, with their control of all four major north-south highways, an opportunity for peace and prosperity. Great wealth flowed into Israel. The prophets' messages reveal, however, that most of the people of the land never enjoyed any of the prosperity. The rich got richer, and the poor got poorer. Jeroboam II took advantage of the power vacuum in the Fertile Crescent and conquered large amounts of the territory of Israel's weaker neighbors. By 750 B.C. Israel's territorial possessions were almost as extensive as they had been under David.

The prophetic messages also reflect that Israel was in the midst of a great religious revival. Unfortunately, it was a revival of the worship of the Canaanite Baals. The people of the land assimilated the worship of Yahweh with that of the Baals. Archaeological excavations have confirmed this, yielding records including a large number of personal names compounded with Baal. Not a single compound name has been found in Judah from this era. The prosperity was superficial and temporary. The prophets announced that apostasy had sealed the doom of the Northern Kingdom. No amount of prosperity could save it.

Increasing instability in the north foreshadowed the coming clouds of judgment. Jeroboam II was succeeded by his son Zechariah (15:8–12). After only six months on the throne, he was assassinated and succeeded by Shallum (15:13–15). He only managed to reign for one month before being assassinated and succeeded by Menahem.

Disaster came in a different form in the south. Azariah of Judah is credited with being a good king. Still, he became proud and burned incense in the temple, so God struck him with leprosy. He became a princely outcast (2 Chron. 26:16). During those latter days of his reign, he was forced to take his son Jotham onto the throne with him as a co-regent. While not as prosperous in those days as her northern sister, neither did Judah become as involved in idolatry.

Just as the people of Israel became less able to defend themselves, the dangers they faced increased. The increasing chaos of the Northern Kingdom was accompanied by the end of civil conflict in Assyria. Internal consolidation allowed them once again to look toward the smaller nations of Palestine, including Israel, as the object of territorial expansion. Assyria humiliated King Menahem of Israel, forcing him to pay massive tribute. To do so he had to tax his people heavily (15:16–22). He was succeeded by his son Pekahiah (15:23–26). Once again, internal chaos took over. Pekah assassinated Pekahiah (15:27–31). In Judah, conditions moved along with more stability, Ahaz succeeding Jotham (15:32–38).

At this point, Judah faced the Syro-Ephraimitic crisis that ultimately brought the end of the Northern Kingdom (16:1–9). The crisis started with a coalition between Syria and Ephraim. Isaiah spoke to it quite specifically, addressing his message to Ahaz of Judah (Isa. 7). In 735 B.C. Pekah of Israel and Rezin of Syria sought to involve Judah in a coalition to prevent Assyria from becoming any stronger. When Ahaz of Judah refused to join, Syria and Ephraim planned to attack Judah. They intended to depose Ahaz and put their own puppet ruler on the throne of Jerusalem. This would bring Judah into their fold. Rejecting Isaiah's advice, Ahaz sent tribute to Assyria with a plea for help. This international intrigue led to the final defeat of Syria in 732 B.C. and the fall of Israel in 722 B.C..

During those final days of Israel, Pekah was assassinated and succeeded by Hoshea (not to be confused with Hosea the prophet), Israel's final king (17:1–5). Samaria's defense proved itself. The mighty Assyrians needed three years to capture the city (17:6–41).

In dealing with captive nations, the Assyrians practiced mass deportation. Removing many Hebrews from Israel, the Assyrians brought in peoples from other conquered nations to settle in their place. These people then, all speaking different languages, could not communicate with one another. From the Assyrian standpoint, this inability of the captive peoples to communicate hindered the possibility of future rebellions. From a Hebrew perspective, this Assyrian policy produced two long-ranging results: (1) intermarriage between the Hebrews left behind in Israel and foreign pagans who had been settled among them. This produced the people who came to be known as Samaritans in the New

Testament era. (2) The end of Israel. Sadly, little Judah now stood alone, the only remainder of David's once great empire.

Part Three. The Divided Monarchy, Judah Alone (18:1—25:30)

Since Judah had asked for and paid tribute to gain Assyrian help in the Syro-Ephraimitic crisis, Assyria did not attack them. Instead, they were little more than an Assyrian vassal. They could take no military initiative and had to send regular tribute to fill the Assyrian treasury.

I. Hezekiah's Accomplishments and Failures (18:1—20:21)

Ahaz was on Judah's throne during Israel's demise. His son Hezekiah inherited a throne not only subservient to Assyria but in the midst of a major religious decay (18:1–12).

Here we face a significant textual problem. The Bible states that Hezekiah began to reign in "the third year of King Hoshea" (18:1). His father Ahaz had begun to reign when he was twenty, in the seventeenth year of Pekah (16:1–2; 2 Chron. 28:1). Since Pekah reigned twenty years, Ahaz would have been twenty-three at the accession of his son Hoshea (15:27). Since Hezekiah began to reign in the third year of Hosea, Ahaz would have been twenty-six when he died. Hezekiah, Ahaz's son, however, was twenty-five at that same time (18:2). A father cannot be only one year older than his son. We admit that we have a serious textual problem and wait for future discoveries or developments to help us deal with our difficulties.

Much of the chronological evidence surrounding Hezekiah's years is confusing. Study leads to the conclusion that Hezekiah began to reign about 715 B.C., though some scholars place him on the throne in 727 B.C. Assyrian attention was directed toward a major Babylonian revolt. This led numerous small kingdoms in the region of Syria-Palestine to begin what were to be abortive revolts against their Assyrian masters. While Hezekiah did not join in those, he apparently did seize on that time as an opportunity for a major religious reform in Judah.

The situation moved along with little change until Sennacherib became king of Assyria in 705 B.C. Once again, Babylon rebelled, joined by the rebellious kings of Ashkelon, Ekron, and Tyre. Judah may have been part of this rebellion. At least, they withheld their annual tribute. In 701 B.C., after having dealt with the more threatening of the revolutionaries, the Assyrian armies marched into Judah (18:13—19:37) They seemed on the verge of destroying the Southern Kingdom just as they had earlier destroyed her northern sister. The taunts of the Rabshakeh of Assyria (chief officer of the Assyrian army) hardened the resistance of the Hebrew people. He threatened to remove them from their land, God's gift. Further, he became more arrogant and rejected the possibility of God's intervention. As a result, Isaiah the prophet sent a message of hope, promising Yahweh's intervention. The Assyrians were miraculously defeated, and their armies withdrew.

Egyptian records of the Assyrian campaign tell about the Assyrian army being overrun by a horde of mice that devoured their bowstrings. Mice and rats are known hosts to fleas, who often carry bubonic plague. God may have used such a visitation to drive the Assyrians back to their own land. Assyria's own boastful records never seem to have recorded a defeat. These records claim that the Assyrians shut Hezekiah up in Jerusalem like a bird in a cage. This was temporarily true. The records also never reported the capture of Jerusalem. This was also true because the Assyrians never captured Jerusalem.

During Hezekiah's preparation for the defense of Jerusalem, he apparently prepared a tunnel to bring water from the pool of Siloam to the city of Jerusalem so the city could better withstand a siege (20:20). This amazing bit of engineering produced a winding tunnel, dug through limestone by two teams of workers beginning at each end. They actually met in the middle almost precisely on target.

A life-threatening illness marked Hezekiah's final days (20:1–21). Once again, God responded to his prayers through the prophet Isaiah, prolonging his life for a time. Of all the kings of Judah, Hezekiah was one of only two who had nothing negative recorded about their relationship with Yahweh. He was remembered as a good king who sought to lead his people back to God.

II.   Apostasy and Reform (21:1— 23:30)

As is often the case, good King Hezekiah's son not only did not follow in his father's footsteps, he became the most evil king ever to reign in Judah (21:1–18). Probably under outside pressure, Manasseh led his nation back to the worship of the ancient gods of Canaan and to the newer gods of Assyria. He even burned one of his sons as a sacrifice to his new gods. An ancient, though nonbiblical, tradition claims that Manasseh tied up Isaiah in a hollow tree and sawed him in two. That tradition may be reflected in Hebrews 11:37. In any case, Manasseh was guilty of oppressing his people violently.

Manasseh ruled longer than any other king of Judah, but was ultimately remembered for his evil. Finally, his son Amon ruled (21:19–26). Obviously he was following in his father's evil path, so after two years his councilors assassinated him. Apparently, they planned to seize the throne for one of their own. Instead, the people of the land executed them and placed Amon's young son on the throne in his place, thus maintaining the Davidic dynasty.

Eight-year-old Josiah brought the innocence of childhood to the throne. Either too young to have been contaminated by the evil of his grandfather and father or too repulsed by their evil, he set out to reform his nation and their faith (22:1–7).

Early in his reform, King Josiah cleansed and refurbished the temple. During that process, "the book of the law" was found (22:8–20). Contemporary Christians find it difficult to comprehend how such Scriptures could be lost. The only copies were made by hand and retained in the temple. The surprising element is that any copies survived during Manasseh's long reign of evil.

When Josiah heard the scroll read, he immediately recognized and accepted it as authoritative Scripture. Seeking a prophetic word for guidance, Josiah began to use the scroll as the basis for an even more thorough reform of the life and faith of his nation (23:1–27). No one is sure of the contents of the scroll found in the temple. It was clearly part of the law (Torah), for that was what it was called. When a list is made of everything that Josiah did following the finding of the scroll, we discover that one Old Testament book, Deuteronomy, commands all of those things. Scholars generally assume that the scroll that became the basis of Josiah's reform was Deuteronomy.

The rest of Josiah's reign was fairly peaceful, until his death in 609 B.C. At that time, Pharaoh Neco sought to go to the aid of Assyria when it was under the attack of Babylon.[7] With a smaller army and no possibility of victory, Josiah sought to halt the advance of the Egyptian army. Seemingly, he sought to prevent the rescue of Assyria, Judah's bitter enemy. He accomplished his pur-

---

7. From this point until the end of the exile, the Babylonians became of major significance for the Hebrews. See"The Babylonians and Chaldeans," *Peoples of Old Testament Times* (Clarendon Press, 1973), 179–96.

pose, but he lost his life in consequence. Thus good king Josiah gave his life attempting to rescue his people from Assyria, their most oppressive enemy. Ironically, wicked Manasseh's father, Hezekiah, and grandson, Josiah, were the only two kings the author of Kings gave no negative marks.

III.   The Last Days of Judah (23:31—25:30)

Following the rather lengthy report of Josiah's reign and reform, the Kings narrative draws rapidly to a close. Jeremiah began his ministry during the early days of Josiah's reign and continued it until after the fall of Jerusalem in 587/86 B.C. His book serves as a valuable resource for anyone seeking to understand all that occurred during the last days of Judah. Furthermore, our understanding of this era is significantly enhanced by knowing what was going on between the major world powers of this era, Egypt, Assyria, and Babylon.

Although well intentioned, the reform of King Josiah was simply a case of too little, too late. Insofar as the general public was concerned, the reform was done too superficially to attract great attention.

Following the defeat of Judah's forces and Josiah's death at Megiddo, Pharaoh Neco arrived too late to help Assyria avoid catastrophic defeat by the Babylonians. In disgust he turned homeward, proceeding through Judah and Jerusalem.

Following Josiah's death, "the people of the land" took Josiah's second son, Jehoahaz, and made him king (23:30–35). Their passing over his older brother, Eliakim, probably indicates that they did not expect him to continue Josiah's policies. (See 23:31,36.) Being unable to punish Josiah, who was already dead, and believing that Jehoahaz would continue the dead king's policies, Neco dispossessed Jehoahaz, carrying him captive to Egypt. In his place, the Egyptian monarch enthroned the older Eliakim, changing his name to Jehoiakim. In addition, Neco levied a massive tax on Judah, probably to reimburse him for the expenses of the military campaign that the armies of Judah had thwarted. Changing the king's name represented Neco's public pronouncement that the Judean king was wholly subservient to his Egyptian master and testifies to the general weakness of Judah at that time.

Egyptian might was on the wane, however. The Babylonian empire was expanding. The Babylonian armies appeared in the region and forced Jehoiakim to become the slave of a new master

(23:36—24:7). For the fiercely independent Judeans, this was not a situation to be endured any longer than necessary. When he was able, Jehoiakim rebelled against Nebuchadnezzar. Unable to respond personally, the Babylonian king used the forces of his vassal kingdoms to harass Judah and Jerusalem.

Just as Nebuchadnezzar finally marched his troops into the region, Jehoiakim died. His eighteen-year-old son, Jehoiachin, ascended the throne (24:8–17). Reigning only three months until the Babylonians arrived, Jehoiachin surrendered to Nebuchadnezzar to spare his beloved Jerusalem the ravages of war. At that time, the young king and the leaders of the nation were carried captive to Babylon, along with many of the temple treasures. The Babylonians placed Mattaniah, Jehoiachin's uncle, on the throne and changed his name to Zedekiah. The name change once again clearly revealed the weakness of Zedekiah and his nation, as well as their subservient relationship to the Babylonian empire.

Zedekiah's unexpected enthronement exemplified a person being forced into a position unprepared and unequipped for the task (24:18—25:7) He is a sad, pathetic figure, a weak man surrounded by counselors stronger than he. Swept along by the pressure of events he could not control, Zedekiah foolishly rebelled against the Babylonians. This was more than Nebuchadnezzar could endure. Once again his armies marched against the Kingdom of Judah and Jerusalem its capital.

The end of the Hebrew experiment with monarchy did not come swiftly, but it came inexorably (25:8–30). After an eighteen month siege, the Babylonian forces overcame Jerusalem, the holy city. The palace, the temple, the major buildings, and the city were destroyed. Excavations in the city of Jerusalem bear mute testimony of the violence of that final onslaught. Ash layers more than a yard thick reveal the horror of the destruction the city endured.

Nebuchadnezzar carried off large numbers of captives and placed a governor over what had now become an outlying province of his empire. In one more abortive attempt at revolt, possibly motivated by frustrated anger, some of the people assassinated Gedaliah, the Babylonian governor. Rather than face the further wrath of Nebuchadnezzar, those who might have been held responsible by the Babylonians fled to Egypt. Judah's glorious political history ended. The monarchy no longer existed.

Meanwhile, the exiles in Babylon were treated with an enlightenment never before found among ancient Near Eastern conquerors. They were free to do their own thing, to worship their own gods in their own way. The only thing they could not do was return home. Babylonians still recognized the captive Jehoiachin as King of Judah, even though he was a king in exile. Eventually when Evil-Merodach ascended the Babylonian throne, the king of Judah was freed from close arrest and allowed to live in the Babylonian palace as a guest of the king.

Message

When we come to the end of Kings, we come not only to the end of a book but to the end of that section of the Hebrew canon known as the former prophets. These six books, Joshua, Judges, 1 and 2 Samuel, and 1 and 2 Kings have also been called the Deuteronomic histories. The message of 1 and 2 Kings is closely bound up with these other books and their inter-relationships.   Four major themes stand out.

First, 1 and 2 Kings, and especially their concluding chapters, demonstrate and proclaim that the curses pronounced in Deuteronomy on infidelity to Israel's covenant with Yahweh have all come to pass, bearing their bitter fruit for the chosen people (Deut. 27:15–26; 28:15–68). Deuteronomy carefully set forth the consequences of disobedience to the law of God.

> But if you will not obey the voice of the Lord your God by diligently observing all his commandments and decrees, which I am commanding you today, then all these curses shall come upon you and overtake you.
>
> The Lord will send upon you disaster, panic, and frustration, . . . until you are destroyed . . . The Lord will cause you to be defeated before your enemies; . . . you shall build a house, but not live in it; you shall plant a vineyard, but not enjoy its fruit. . . . Your sons and daughters shall be given to another people, while you look on; you will strain your eyes looking for them all day but be powerless to do anything. A people whom you do not known shall eat up the fruit of your ground and of all your labors.
>
> The Lord will bring you, and the king whom you set over you, to a nation that neither you nor your ancestors have known; . . . You shall have sons and daughters, but they shall not be yours; for they shall go into captivity. (Deut. 28:15, 20, 25, 30, 32–33, 36, 41)

The message is clear and certain: disobedience and infidelity has costly consequences. Sin will result in judgment.

A second teaching is not directly proclaimed since the events of Israel's history did not provide a vehicle for it. Still, an indirect proclamation of hope rings through. Since Israel's disobedience resulted in judgment, these books proclaim that *what God promises, God does.* In addition to its curses, Deuteronomy also offered promises of goodness and mercy. The fulfillment of judgment offered hope to Israel. God was, and is, trustworthy. Deuteronomy also teaches that God cares. He is concerned with what His people do. The long wait to punish Israel's and Judah's sins shows God's patient care.

Perhaps the third message of 1 and 2 Kings is the most important. The ancient Near East shared the belief that the defeat of any nation meant that their god or gods had been defeated. The proclamation of these books is to the contrary. The sovereign God of Israel was not defeated when Israel was defeated. Instead, He had defeated Israel. He controlled the enemy armies and used them as His agents of judgment. This message was simple. Israel had been defeated. God was still sovereign.

The fourth and final message of these two books calls our attention to the prophets who were active through the events recorded. When leaders go astray and people willfully follow them into sin, God still has His spokespersons on the scene to proclaim His message to those who are involved. He always calls His people back. Almost hidden in the background of the ministries of the prophets who spoke so boldly was Yahweh's affirmation to the great Elijah: a multitude of the people of the land still remained faithful, even in apostate Israel (1 Kings 19:18). Many quietly went about their business, serving Yahweh the God of Israel. That offers hope.

Questions for Review and Reflection

1. What important events occurred in 931, 853, 722, and 587/86 B.C.?

2. Distinguish between relative chronology and absolute chronology. Why are both important for writing the history of Israel? Define co-regency and explain its importance for one who writes a history of Israel. What difference does it make to you if you can or cannot give an absolute date for an event in Israel's history?

3. If you were an Israelite in exile in Babylon, how would you answer the taunts of Babylonian captors wanting to be entertained with songs of Zion (Ps. 137) and laughing

at your worship because your weak God had suffered defeat?

4. How can one hold to a promise to David and a messianic hope when the Bible's own history says David's ruling line came to an end in 586 B.C.?

5. Use Kings to provide illustrations as you write a one page definition of history and history writing. What part do historical facts play? What part does human interpretation play? What part does divine activity play?

6. How would you answer a classmate who claims that history is a closed system without room for God and His actions in it?

Bibliography

DeVries, Simon John. *1 Kings*. Vol. 10, *Word Biblical Commentary*. Waco: Word, 1985.

Hobbs, T. R. *2 Kings*. Vol. 13, *Word Biblical Commentary*. Waco: Word, 1985.

Jones, Gwilym H. *1 and 2 Kings*. *New Century Bible Commentary*. Grand Rapids: Eerdmans, 1984.

Nelson, Richard D. *First and Second Kings*. Atlanta: John Knox, 1987.

Traylor, John H. *1 & 2 Kings, 2 Chronicles*. Vol. 6, *Layman's Bible Book Commentary*. Nashville: Broadman Press, 1981.

Chapter 7

The Books of
1 and 2 Chronicles

The long genealogy with which 1 and 2 Chronicles begin often leads readers to stop at that point, moving on to more interesting and understandable books. Those who persist beyond that block of material run into frequent references to obscure temple rituals as well as to the detailed assignments of the Levites and priests. This often causes them to move from these books to more easily understood and appreciated materials.

Such feelings are understandable, but failing to read and consider 1 and 2 Chronicles leaves the reader impoverished in grasping the overall message of the Old Testament history books. The situation would be essentially the same if readers of the Gospels decided to base their understanding of Jesus wholly on Mark or John while ignoring the material of Matthew and Luke. Chronicles focuses on the same historical era and events considered in Joshua through 2 Kings, but from a significantly different perspective. That perspective is essential if we are going to achieve the fullest possible understanding of those events and of their meaning for the people of Israel

The Hebrew name for 1 and 2 Chronicles is "The Events of the Days." The Septuagint calls them "The Things Passed Over," apparently referring to the data omitted from 1 and 2 Samuel and 1 and 2 Kings.

Glossary	
ben	This Hebrew word literally means "son" but can mean any descendant of someone else.
Genealogy	A family record of ancestors and their signficance.
Redactor	An editor or one who revises and adapts material prior to publication.
Talmud	A collection of rabbinic records

Place in the Canon, Date, and Authorship

Issues of placement, date, and authorship of 1 and 2 Chronicles must be approached in connection with the problem of unity and theological perspective. These two books, along with Ezra and Nehemiah, seem to have a consistent approach to Hebrew history, although a different one from that of the Deuteronomic histories of Joshua, Judges, 1 and 2 Samuel, and 1 and 2 Kings. Chronicles appears to have a primary concern with the law of Moses and particularly with its rituals, with the worship in the temple of Jerusalem, and with the work of the priests and Levites. This has led interpreters to call these books, along with Ezra and Nehemiah, the Priestly-Levitical histories.

The break between 1 and 2 Chronicles is more natural and logical than the break between 1 and 2 Samuel or that between 1 and 2 Kings. This might indicate separate authors of different books, but the vocabulary, style, interests, and concerns of the two Books of Chronicles seem to be identical. Scholars, therefore, generally assume that these two books were written by the same person. The only other conclusion would be that 1 and 2 Chronicles were put into their present form by one editor. We begin this study, therefore, with the assumption that these two books are a unit and should be studied as such.

In our English canon Chronicles follows immediately after 1 and 2 Kings. In the Hebrew Bible they form the last two books of the entire Scriptures, bringing that canon to an end. That location is important for our overall understanding of the canon of the Old

Testament. Jesus, in His scathing denunciation of the Pharisaic spirit, condemned their absence of love for God's servants by pronouncing them guilty:

> So that upon you may come all the righteous blood shed on earth, from the blood of righteous Abel to the blood of Zechariah . . . whom you murdered between the sanctuary and the altar. (Matt. 23:35)

Abel's death is the first murder in the Bible, while Zechariah's is the last recorded in 2 Chronicles (Gen. 4:8; 2 Chron. 24:21). Since 2 Chronicles was the last book in the Hebrew Bible, Jesus' reference was essentially pointing to all the murders from the beginning to the end of the canon. This shows that the Hebrew canon was completed and in its final form by the time of Jesus.

Chronicles were relocated in the Septuagint or earliest Greek translation and consequently in the English Bible. This was most likely due to the subject matter. Editors of the Greek translation apparently sought to bring the various history books together in one place in the canon.

To establish the date of the writing of 1 and 2 Chronicles, we note that the book ends with the account of the edict of Cyrus. Written about 539 B.C., this allowed the Jews exiled in Babylon to return home to Jerusalem and rebuild their temple (2 Chron. 36:22–23). Obviously, the book was completed after that edict was issued. Further, the genealogies indicate that the final author or editor was familiar with at least five generations following Zerubbabel (1 Chron. 3:19–24). He lived during the rebuilding of the temple between 520 and 516 B.C. (Hag. 2:2). Five generations following that would bring the final writing or editing at least to 400 B.C. and possibly later.

The authorship of 1 and 2 Chronicles is a more difficult problem. The Talmud credits Ezra the scribe with writing Chronicles, Ezra, and Nehemiah. The common authorship of all four books seemed to be apparent to them. Ezra's identification as both a priest and a scribe made him a logical candidate. We do not know whether they received such a tradition from some other source or created it. The same reasons, when coupled with this Talmudic tradition, have led a number of contemporary interpreters to come to the same conclusion.

Recently, several scholars compared the text of Ezra and Nehemiah with the narrative of Chronicles. They found Ezra and Nehemiah stuffy and uninspiring in style compared to the

Chronicles narrative after the genealogies. Chronicles shows a distinct flair for vivid and imaginative phrases. Most modern scholars believe that while 1 and 2 Chronicles probably had a different author (or authors) than did Ezra and Nehemiah, the four books were probably put into their final form by a common editor. The concerns and issues of all of them are the same, but the style and vocabulary are different.[1]

In any case, the authors and final editor of 1 and 2 Chronicles remain unknown. Whoever wrote or edited these books were obviously concerned with the issues of Israel's worship, as well as with their behavior. Further, the intense interest shown in the Levites and in the temple make it probable that both the authors and the editor(s) were from the tribe of Levi and served at the temple of Jerusalem. Most likely the author and editor of Chronicles were among the temple Levites of Jerusalem and wrote between 450 and 350 B.C.

Organization

The organization of 1 and 2 Chronicles leads us to several significant issues:

I. Sources the Authors Used

While scholars have theorized that many Old Testament books were drawn from earlier sources, no book of the Old Testament cites as many sources as Chronicles. Among them are:

1. the Book of the Kings of Israel and Judah (2 Chron. 35:27; 36:8).

2. the Book of the Kings of Judah and Israel (2 Chron. 16:11; 25:26; 28:26; 32:32).

3. the Book of the Kings of Israel (1 Chron. 9:1; 2 Chron. 20:34).

4. a Commentary on the Book of Kings (2 Chron. 24:27).

---

1. For the relationship of Chronicles, Ezra, and Nehemiah, see Peter R. Ackroyd, "Chronicles-Ezra-Nehemiah: the concept of Unity," *Beiheft zur die Zeitschrift für die alttestamentliche Wissenschaft* 100, 189-201; S. Japhet,"The Relationship between Chronicles and Ezra-Nehemiah," *Vetus Testamentum* Supplement XLIII, 1992, 298-313; H. G. M. Williamson, "Did the Author of Chronicles Also Write the Books of Ezra and Nehemiah?" *Bible Review* III (1987), 56-59; David Talshir, "A Reinvestigation of the Linguistic Relationship Between Chronicles and Ezra-Nehemiah," *Vetus Testamentum* 38 (1988), 165-93.

5. the Chronicles of Samuel the Seer (1 Chron. 29:29).

6. the Chronicles of Nathan the Prophet (1 Chron. 29:29).

7. the History of Nathan the Prophet (2 Chron. 9:29).

8. the Chronicles of Gad the Seer (1 Chron. 29:29).

9. the Prophecy of Ahijah the Shilonite (2 Chron. 9:29).

10. the Visions of Iddo the Seer (2 Chron. 9:29).

11. the Chronicles of Shemaiah the Prophet (2 Chron. 12:15).

12. the Chronicles of Iddo the Seer (2 Chron. 12:15).

13. the Story of the Prophet Iddo (2 Chron. 13:22).

14. a Writing of Isaiah the Prophet (2 Chron. 26:22).

15. the Chronicles of the Seers (2 Chron. 33:19).

16. the Chronicles of King David (1 Chron. 27:24).

17. the Directions of David (2 Chron. 35:4).

18. the Directions of Solomon (2 Chron. 35:4).

19. a lament by Jeremiah (2 Chron. 35:25).

20. the Law in the Book of Moses (2 Chron. 25:4; 35:12).

21. the Law of the Lord (1 Chron. 16:40; 2 Chron. 31:3; 35:26).

22. the Law of Moses (1 Chron. 23:18).

23. a writing from the hand of the Lord (1 Chron. 28:19).

Admittedly, some of these citations may be designating the same work by two or more variant references. For example, the Book of the Kings of Israel and Judah and the Book of the Kings of Judah and Israel may be the same work. On the other hand, even granting this assumption, we are still left with a large number of earlier sources specifically identified by the author(s) of Chronicles. Most, if not all, of these sources are not available to us. At the same time, the fact they were available to the original readers of 1 and 2 Chronicles should give us confidence in the accuracy with which the Chronicler used them. He would not have cited them so casually if comparison of his writing with the sources cited could have embarrassed him. The Chronicler also quoted from other Old Testament passages that he did not bother to cite. Note the three Psalms he quoted in 1 Chronicles 16 (Pss. 96:1–13; 105:1–15; 106:47–48).

II. The Historiography Revealed in Chronicles

As with all other biblical histories, these two books focus their primary attention not so much on the events that occurred as on what those events meant. For them the real issue was what Yahweh was doing in those events.

In a significant change from what we have found in earlier biblical books, in 1 and 2 Chronicles the history of the people of Israel was assessed on the authority of a written law. Over and over again, the authors referred not so much to what God said through His prophetic intermediaries as to what was written in the Torah (1 Chron. 16:40; 2 Chron. 23:18; 25:4; 30:5,18; 31:3; 34:21,24,31; 35:12,26). This feature became the essential characteristic of the historiography of Chronicles.

III. The Historical Focus of the Books

The six books of the Deuteronomic history focused on the Hebrew people from the time of their entry into Canaan under Joshua until their exile following the destruction of Jerusalem by the Babylonians. Chronicles, on the other hand, began their narrative with Adam and continued it until King Cyrus allowed the Hebrews to return from the Babylonian exile in 539 B.C. Furthermore, during the era of the divided monarchy, 1 and 2 Kings followed the history of both Israel and Judah. Chronicles followed the history of Judah alone, mentioning Israel and its kings only where they were significantly involved with what was going on in Judah.

While we do not know precisely why the Chronicler omitted Israel from his narrative, two possibilities have been suggested. Perhaps these books were written so long after the destruction of the Northern Kingdom that Israel was no longer of major interest or concern to the Hebrew people. On the other hand, the focus of Chronicles is so clearly on what happened to the temple of Jerusalem, the capital of the Southern Kingdom, that the Northern Kingdom simply was never directly involved.

IV. Historical Reliability

Many scholars compare Chronicles with the Gospel of John. These scholars say both books were written to communicate faith and not history. The reasons for making this suggestion have come from at least three different kinds of data.

First, problems are seen with the numbers given for the size of Israel's armies. King Jehoshaphat, for example, is credited with having an army with five major contingents numbering 300,000 men, 280,000 men, 200,000 men, 200,000 men, and 180,000 men. This totals 1,160,000 men (2 Chron. 17:14–18). At the same time Jehoshaphat is described as being hopelessly outnumbered by his enemies (2 Chron. 20:12,15). Data outside Chronicles indicates that no enemy of Judah ever had an army even remotely approaching such a size. A possible solution for this problem may be that the Hebrew word *eleph*, which originally meant "a thousand," can also refer to "a fighting unit," such as a squad or a company.[2] This would reduce the army of Jehoshaphat to 1,160 fighting units and thus alleviate the problem with the numbers here.

Second, problems exist in the Chronicler's listing of Israel's financial records. One example will suffice. David is said to have amassed 100,000 talents of gold and one million talents of silver. Given our knowledge of the value of a talent of either gold or silver, this treasure would have amounted to billions of dollars, a figure far in excess of the treasure that any kingdom of the era ever possessed. At the same time, we must admit that we are not sure what the actual weight of a talent in David's time was. Further, the Old Testament frequently used numbers as symbols rather than as specific quantities. This is particularly true of multiples of ten. This may have been the case here. Our lack of detailed knowledge of the era makes it impossible to make a definitive judgment of our data.

Third, questions of the historical reliability of the Chronicler relate to events for which no other evidence exists either in or out of the Old Testament. Early interpreters of Chronicles were very skeptical of such accounts. Recently discovered records of the eras involved have, on occasion, demonstrated that some of these events happened as described. Further, the abundant citations to ancient sources given by the Chronicler should also give us confidence in the accuracy with which such sources were used.[3]

---

2. For another place where this understanding of *'eleph* helps in understanding a difficult text, see Numbers 2, as well as the material in J. J. Owens, "Numbers," *The Broadman Bible Commentary*, vol. 2 (Broadman Press, 1970), 84–85.

3. A more detailed discussion of the Chronicler's historical reliability can be found in Clyde Francisco, "1–2 Chronicles," *The Broadman Bible Commentary*, vol. 3 (Broadman Press, 1970), 300–01; the most recent study is S. Japhet, *I & II Chronicles*, the Old Testament Library (Louisville: Westminster/John Knox, 1993), 1-49; Compare D. M. Howard, Jr., *An Introduction to the Old Testament Historical Books* (Chicago: Moody Press, 1993), 236-69.

We cannot state that all of the information given by the Chronicler has been proven to be true. On the other hand, much that had been questioned has been affirmed. Further, the major gaps in our knowledge of the era make assertions of historical unreliability unreliable themselves.

V. The Focus or Thrust of the Work

The issue is usually raised with the question: why do we have a second account of the history of the Hebrew people? The answer can be found in noting that we have a similar situation when it comes to the Gospels. Each adds to our understanding of the events in the life of Jesus. At the same time, each also gives a new thrust to our understanding of the meaning of Jesus' life. The same seems to be true here. The Chronicler viewed God's dealings with the Hebrew people from a different perspective and reinterpreted the message of those dealings for a new generation and era, applying it to the needs of Yahweh's people after 400 B.C. The focus of 1 and 2 Chronicles is on the centrality of the service of God in the life of God's people.

We must not contrast the work of the author of Kings with that of the author of Chronicles, seeking to say one is right and the other wrong. Both were right. Their perspectives were different, and the messages that they proclaimed were complementary of each other. We must not choose to study one approach or the other. It takes both approaches to get the full message of the events.

Having considered the various fundamental issues in the study of 1 and 2 Chronicles, we are ready to examine an outline of their contents. As in the outlines of 1 and 2 Samuel and 1 and 2 Kings, we shall not identify the specific book in the biblical references given here, since we are moving through them from beginning to end.

Content Outline

(Since we have dealt with the basic historical material presented in our study of Samuel and Kings, this outline is not in the detail of those given earlier. Further, the historical table used with 1 and 2 Kings is not repeated.

    I. Genealogies from Adam to the temple servants (1:1—9:44)

        A. From Adam to the sons of Israel (1:1—2:2)

    B. A period of highs and lows (23:1—32:33)

       1. Joash and his reforms (23:1—24:27)

       2. Amaziah's apostasy (25:1–28)

       3. Uzziah's success and failures (26:1–23)

       4. Jotham's reign (27:1–9)

       5. Ahaz's tragic compromises (28:1–27)

       6. Hezekiah's reforms (29:1—32:33)

    C. The rush to exile (33:1—36:21)

       1. Manasseh's evil reign (33:1–20)

       2. Amon follows Manasseh's policy (33:21–25)

       3. Josiah's great reform (34:1—35:27)

       4. Judah's final decay and defeat under Jehoahaz, Jehoiakim, Jehoiachin, and Zedekiah (36:1–21)

    D. Cyrus orders release from exile (36:22–23)

Summary of Contents

In this section we will primarily describe passages where Chronicles takes a significantly different approach, makes a unique emphasis, or introduces an event not recorded in Samuel and Kings. In this way we will perceive Chronicles' basic thrust. This approach lets us emphasize the very differences that caused this material to be written and canonized.

I. Genealogies from Adam to the Temple Servants (1:1—9:44)

The content outline shows that 1 Chronicles has the most extensive set of genealogies preserved in one place in the Bible. Four features help contemporary readers grasp the significance of genealogies for Israel and for us.

- The ancient Hebrews' use of the word *ben*, normally translated as *son*.—This term is not limited to one who is simply the immediate son of a parent, but it is used almost as frequently for "grandson," a "great-grandson," or a descendant. Jesus is called "Son of David," even though many generations separated the two. Reconstructing a detailed and accurate genealogy involves checking the details of these genealogies with those of other genealogies and with narrative literature.

- The extreme importance of lineage for the Hebrews.— Establishing one's lineage provided a sense of identity and established one's portion among the people of God. God had distributed the land to the tribes and families of Israel (Josh. 13—19). God expected that land to remain in the family line. The laws of Jubilee as well as occasional narratives call this to our attention. Each Israelite had to know who was in the family line. Conversely, Israel had to know to which family line any particular individual belonged. Keeping genealogies ensured a tribe's continued membership in God's people and maintained a family's hold on its ancestral land.

- The concentration on the families of Levi and David.— Chronicles gives relatively large space to the tribe of Levi and to the family of David, even though the latter was not a tribe (2:3—3:24; 6:1—81; 9:1—34). This alerts the reader to the importance for Chronicles of the offices of priest and king.

- The genealogy of the Levites not only gives their heritage but their functions and responsibilities in the temple service.—This peculiar emphasis means that Chronicles has a special interest in the temple and its service. By the time of the Chronicler, the Davidic kingdom had ceased to exist. The line of David was the foundation of Israel's future hope. Yahweh's covenant with David promised that one day the kingdom would be reestablished. Hope for the individual and the nation remained tied to the hope for David.

Of more relevance for the author and for the Hebrew people, only one thing gave them a sense of immediate national identity — the worship of Yahweh. Only the Levitical Priesthood could ensure proper worship. The Levites' genealogy gave the priests and Israel their present identity and function in the kingdom of God. Only as they properly fulfilled their responsibility could Israel continue to exist. Thus these two genealogies gave the people of Israel their sense of present relationship to God and of their ultimate hope in the fulfillment of His promises. The attention paid to these genealogies at the very beginning alerts us to the emphasis of the rest of the book.

II. David's Reign (10:1—29:30)

Compared with the contents of 1 and 2 Samuel and 1 Kings, several features stand out in the Chronicler's report of David's reign. First, most of the struggles and conflicts between David and Saul are either omitted or are significantly modified. Saul's entire reign covers only fourteen verses (10:1–14).

Second, all the details of David's outlaw days under Saul are omitted, including his time as a servant of Achish, the Philistine ruler of Gath.

Third, David's adultery with Bathsheba and his murder of Uriah are passed over with only a mention of David's having remained home when his armies went forth to battle the Ammonites (20:1).

Fourth, David's problems as a father are ignored. Amnon's rape of Tamar, Absalom's murder of Amnon, and Absalom's rebellion are all left out. (Compare 2 Sam. 13:1–29; 15:1—18:33.) In addition, David's ongoing problems with his nephew Joab are also omitted.

Fifth, in a theological development, the Chronicler attributed David's census of Israel to the temptation of Satan rather than God's word (21:1; compare 2 Sam. 24). Here we apparently have the only Old Testament reference to Satan as the personal name of the evil one. In Numbers 22:22,32; 1 Samuel 29:4; 2 Samuel 19:22; 1 Kings 5:4; 11:14,23,25; Psalm 109:6; and probably in Job 1—2 and Zechariah 3:2 the Hebrew term should be translated as a common noun, "accuser" or "adversary."

Sixth, David's connection with the temple of Solomon appears in far more detail than in Samuel or Kings. The purchase of Arunah's (Ornan's) threshing floor and the listing of the enormous treasures collected and turned over to Solomon to build the temple are given with great detail (21:18—22:19).

Finally, the Chronicler spent five chapters dealing with David's organization and regulation of temple worship (23:1—27:34) Details of David's civil and religious administration are commingled, clearly demonstrating the theocratic nature of the Hebrew monarchy. God was the ruler. David represented Him. What David did in politics and in religion were acts of God's designated earthly representative.

III. Solomon's Reign (1:1—9:31)

The single-mindedness of the Chronicler is equally clear as he writes about Solomon. Items of history that did not help communicate his central message, he simply omitted. He did not attempt to reconstruct history. To the contrary, the inspired writer used the history of God's relations with Israel as a vehicle for revelation. He communicated how God works out His Divine purposes in the human sphere. The author's method of writing was his way of keeping extraneous human details from intruding on the Divine message.

As with David, the presentation of Solomon illustrates the Chronicler's method and purpose.

First, he provides no record of the human struggle over the successor to David. For the Chronicler, neither the rebellion of Absalom nor the intrigues of Adonijah could intrude on God's purpose for Solomon to follow David on the throne. The author did not say or imply that these other things did not happen. He indicated that *ultimately such human actions did not matter.* What did matter was that Solomon's accession to the throne fulfilled God's purpose. Thus, for him, nothing that intruded on that process was worth reporting.

Second, the Chronicler omitted the long list of Solomon's sins and administrative failures found in Kings (1 Kings 11). Again, the Chronicler made no attempt at a cover-up. The audience knew these things clearly, the Kings' record being well known. These events simply did not fit into the message he was communicating.

Third, Solomon built the temple of Jerusalem with the treasures and major supplies David had gathered and according to the plans he had laid out. Solomon only had to fulfill his father's dreams and plans. The Chronicler was not as concerned with glorifying either David or Solomon as in glorifying the temple and Jerusalem, its seat. Both David and Solomon are presented only as agents in the establishment of God's temple, God's city, and God's kingdom on earth. The focus is on Yahweh's fulfillment of His purposes, not on the deeds of His servants.

IV. Judah from the Division to the Restoration (10:1—36:23)

Following the death of Solomon, the kingdom divided. Contrary to the pattern found in 1 and 2 Kings, from this point Chronicles follows only the story of the Southern Kingdom of Judah. The Northern Kingdom of Israel and her rulers receive mention only where they interacted with Judah in influencing Judah's faithfulness and loyalty to Yahweh and to the temple and the worship practices found there.

The Chronicler dealt with David and Solomon, the founders of the dynasty, differently from the way he dealt with their successors. With David and Solomon, he emphasized almost totally the way they worked with one another and with God in building the temple of Jerusalem and in providing for and regulating the worship in the temple. Once Chronicles notes that the temple had been finished and the worship of Yahweh established, the remaining kings in Jerusalem receive different treatment. In most cases their sins were catalogued showing how they departed from the faith of David and Solomon by rebelling against the law of Yahweh, including the rituals of the temple. Thus they brought judgment on themselves and their kingdom (12:1; 16:12; 21:6; 22:3; 25:14; 26:16; 28:1–4,22,25; 33:2–9; 33:22; 36:5,12–13). Following this long list of rebellious rulers came the final judgment. Yahweh took away from Judah His best gift: the temple and His worship (36:17–20, especially v.19) We need to remember that the temple and its rituals symbolized Yahweh's presence in the midst of His people. Yet not only did He take away His gift to the people, He also took the people away from the land He had given.

The second outstanding feature in the Chronicler's record of this era is the emphasis on God guiding Judah's history by His Word. This shows up in three ways, the most obvious being the ministry of the prophets. Over again the Chronicler pointed out how prophets were raised up in critical times to confront the kings and their people with God's demands (12:5; 15:1; 16:7; 19:2; 20:37; 21:12; 25:7; 34:22). The prophets are more abundant in Chronicles than in Kings, but the people generally ignored them. Considering the Chronicler's emphasis on the prophetic word, we are struck by the fact that Elijah is only mentioned once by the Chronicler and Elisha is not mentioned at all (2 Chron. 21:12). This probably resulted from their ministries being carried out primarily in the Northern Kingdom.

In addition to the prophetic word, the Chronicler pointed out that God sought to guide the kings and their people through His Law (12:1; 24:18; 25:4; 31:3,21; 34:14; 35:12,26) This by itself was not enough. Repeatedly, Chronicles emphasizes the involvement of priests and Levites in interpreting and applying the word of God to the world situation in which they lived (11:13; 17:7–9; 19:8–11; 20:13–17; 23:1–11; 24:11,20; 26:17–18; 29:4–19,25–28,34–35; 30:16–22; 31:2,12–19; 34:12–13; 35:10–19). Although emphasizing their work, the Chronicler was also straightforward in pointing out the sins and failure of the Levites. They were God's servants, but they were still human.

The Chronicler's emphasis through his report of the work of both Levites and prophets was consistent. The people of Israel needed to know God had sought to guide them throughout this period of dissolution and downfall. He had never abandoned them. The failure was not His but theirs.

The third significant feature of the Chronicler's record of the history of Judah relates to the reign of Manasseh. In Kings, wicked Manasseh is not reported to have any redeeming features. Chronicles, on the other hand, reported that he was carried as a captive to Babylon, where he repented of his evil and received Yahweh's forgiveness (33:10–20). Following his repentance, he was released and spent the later part of his reign showing that his repentance was genuine.

A fourth feature of Chronicles, while not of major historical significance, fits with the emphasis on the priests, the Levites, and the Law. The exile, portrayed in Kings as pure judgment, in Chronicles has the added dimension of giving the land a sabbath rest of seventy years (36:21). The land, having been so abused by the people of God, needed a sabbath rest from them. What a tragic commentary on their history.

The final significant feature is that Chronicles does not end with the exile, as did Kings. Chronicles concludes with the edict of Cyrus ordering the Hebrews to return and rebuild the temple in Jerusalem (36:23). Thus the Chronicler ended his work on a note of hope. This is especially significant when we remember that in the Hebrew Bible, Chronicles is the last book of their canon. In addition, what is missing gives a forward look. The temple was to be rebuilt and the worship of Yahweh reestablished, and that was wonderful. The kingdom of David was not reestablished at that time. That was still in their future, not to be accomplished until the ministry of great David's greater Son. It was that ultimate hope to which the people could still look.

Message

Because the content of Chronicles is similar to that of Kings, people do not expect a new message or emphasis. The existence of this second source should alert us to look for new emphases and

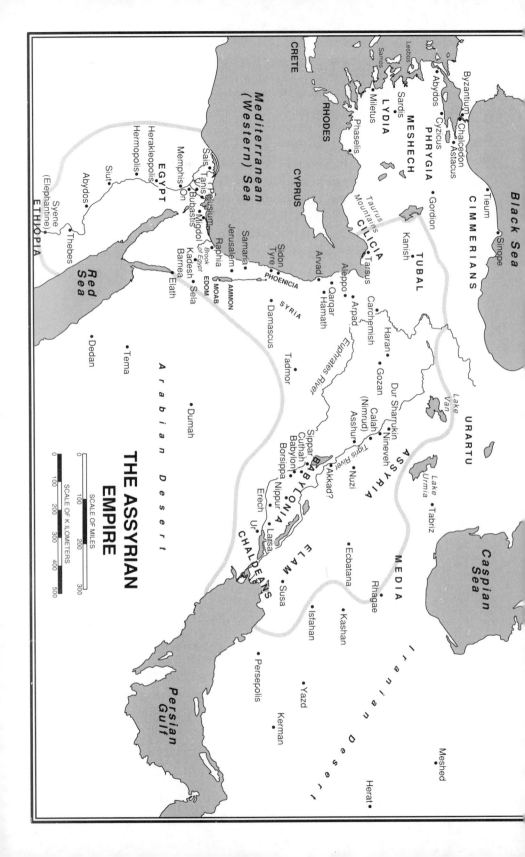

new faith proclamations. They are here in abundance. The following seem to be the main ones.

1. Worship is of utmost importance for the people of God. He expects us to approach Him in a worthy manner and in a worthy environment. Offering anything less than our best in worship is an indication that we do not value God as of ultimate importance.

2. Faithful and proper worship is no substitute for obedience to God. He expects His people to give Him their absolute loyalty and faithfulness in all of life.

3. The message drawn from God's mighty acts in history will change with new situations. His sovereignty does not change, but the application of the lessons of the past do change as present situations alter.

4. God's written Law is authoritative on His people. More emphasis is placed here on that written law than in any other book of the Bible. That Law may be interpreted to us by His servants, and it may be interpreted to us by His Spirit. Regardless, its authority is absolute and must be the basis of life for God's people.

5. The heritage of God's people is important. God's promises come to those who follow Him as a part of that heritage and need to be treasured as such. This shows up particularly in the heritage of David, for it is in great David's greater Son that God's Kingdom is ultimately fulfilled.

6. Being God's servant does not negate our humanity and certainly does not make us sinless. Therefore, we need to recognize that sin and disobedience always bring judgment. Sin has consequences that cannot be escaped.

7. Beyond humanity's sin and beyond God's judgment, God's hope always stands. He will keep His promises and ultimately establish His kingdom.

Questions for Review and Reflection

1. List major differences in content and method between the author of Kings and the writer of Chronicles.

2. Explain the theological and historical importance of the presence of Chronicles alongside Kings in the Bible.

3. Why should a person today study the genealogies in Scripture?

4. How can you learn something for your life from the Chronicler's emphasis on Jewish law, temple worship, and Levitical service?

5. Choose David, Solomon, Rehoboam, Josiah, Hezekiah, or Manasseh. Compare the accounts of Chronicles and Kings. Describe the similarities and the differences. What do you learn from these about the nature of Scripture and about the nature of life under God.

Bibliography

Braun, Roddy. *1 Chronicles.* Vol. 14, *Word Biblical Commentary.* Waco: Word 1986.

DeVries, Simon John. *1 and 2 Chronicles.* (Forms of Old testament Literature) Grand Rapids: Eerdmans, 1989.

Dillard, Raymond Bryan. *2 Chronicles.* Vol. 15, *Word Biblical Commentary.* Waco: Word, 1987.

Japhet, S. *I & II Chronicles.* (Old Testament Library) Louisville: Westminster/John Knox Press, 1993.

McConville, J. G. *I & II Chronicles.* Philadelphia: Westminster, 1984.

Merrill, Eugene H. *1, 2 Chronicles: Bible Study Commentary.* Grand Rapids: Lamplighter, 1988.

Williamson, H. G. M. "1 and 2 Chronicles" (New Century Bible) Grand Rapids: Eerdmans, 1982.

Chapter 8

The Books of
Ezra and Nehemiah

The Books of Ezra and Nehemiah are distinctively related to 1 and 2 Chronicles. They share numerous features that are either not found, or are not found to the same degree, in any other historical book in the Bible. Most scholars assume that these four books were originally a part of a common collection. At least they share such a common outlook on Hebrew history as to suggest a common editor or redactor. Since we concluded that 1 and 2 Chronicles could be considered to be a "Priestly-Levitical" approach to the history of the Hebrew people, we can begin our study of the Books of Ezra and Nehemiah with the same assumption. They, too, are a part of the Priestly-Levitical history.

Glossary

Aramaic	The language of the Syrian nation used by the Hebrew people following the time of the exile and on through that of the New Testament.

Glossary	
Cup-bearer	A highly honored and trusted position, being one who literally tasted the wine for a king, checking both to be sure it was not poisoned and that it was fit for a king to drink.
Exile	The time when many Hebrews lived in Babylon, having been deported following Babylon's conquest of Judah, extending from 587/86 to 539 B.C.
Medo-Persian Empire	Came to power after a coalition of Medes and Persians from the mountains to the northeast of the Mesopotamian Valley overthrew Babylon in 539 B.C.
Scribe	One of the professionals who was trained to read and write and who copied the Scriptures to preserve and pass them on.

Place in the Canon, Date, and Authorship

The Books of Ezra and Nehemiah (from this point on, the two books together shall be called Ezra/Nehemiah), are located in different places in different scriptural canons. In the Hebrew canon, they precede 1 and 2 Chronicles. This may represent a theological intention to end the canon with Chronicles and its note of hope, or it may be the accident of canonical preservation. In the Septuagint, they are located after 1 and 2 Chronicles, probably because they carry on the story of the Hebrews following the return Cyrus ordered (Ezra 1:1–4). This Greek translation also combines these two books into one, 1 Esdras. In our English Bibles, they are also located immediately after 1 and 2 Chronicles, but they are divided into two books.

Both books were written in Hebrew, with the exception that Ezra 4:8—6:18 and 7:12–26 were written in Aramaic. Although we cannot be certain why this was done, it appears that the first section was copied from the official records of Persia, while the second section seems to be a copy of a letter written by the Persian king, Artaxerxes. These could both have been originally written in Aramaic and were simply copied as written. That the author felt free to leave them in their original language, rather than translating them into Hebrew, shows that Aramaic was understood by the Hebrews in the time when these books were written.

The features Ezra/Nehemiah have in common with 1 and 2 Chronicles have led numerous scholars to suggest that they had a *common* author. This belief is reflected in ancient Hebrew traditions that insist Ezra wrote all four of these books. Even to those reading them in English and to anyone reading them in Hebrew, differences exist between these books. The pedantic and stuffy nature of the narrative found in Ezra/Nehemiah is different from the vivid and active stories found in much of 1 and 2 Chronicles. The difference between Chronicles and Ezra/Nehemiah seems to force the conclusion that two different authors were involved. Their similarities and common interests in the Law, the ritual, and the activities of the priests and Levites make it as probable that they eventually were edited and put into their final forms by a common editor. The author remains unknown.

The date of the writing of Ezra/Nehemiah hinges on the identity of the King Artaxerxes under whom Ezra and Nehemiah served. They may have served under either Artaxerxes I (Longimanus), who reigned from 464 to 423 B.C. or Artaxerxes II (Mnemon), who reigned from 404 to 359 B.C. Obviously, the writing of these books could not have been finished until the ministries of Ezra and Nehemiah were completed.

Organization

Interpreters have raised several issues relating to the Books of Ezra/Nehemiah. These issues must at least be understood before we can consider the overall content and organization.

Like 1 and 2 Chronicles, Ezra/Nehemiah focuses on what was written in the Law (Ezra 3:2,4; 6:14,18; 7:6,10,12,14,21,25,26; 9:10,14; 10:3; Neh. 1:7; 8:1–3,5,8,14,18; 9:3,26,34; 10:29; 13:1,3). In addition, these books focus attention on the work of David and Solomon in establishing the temple and its service, and place an even greater emphasis on the work of the priests and the Levites. Further, although the work of prophets is found here, it does not receive the same emphasis we saw in 1 and 2 Chronicles.

The two most significant issues related to the study of Ezra/Nehemiah are (1) which historical era do these books cover and (2) what is the chronological order of the ministries of Ezra and

Nehemiah.[1] Ezra/Nehemiah begins with the edict of Cyrus allowing the Jews to return to their homeland after Babylon's defeat by the Medo-Persian coalition. The narrative covers approximately one-and-a-half centuries, until near the end of the Persian empire. The basic problem we face when we consider this era is our overall ignorance of this period.

When we dealt with the history of the Hebrew monarchy, we were afforded a luxurious abundance of historical evidence from the major kingdoms of that period. In addition to the evidence of Egyptian, Assyrian, and Babylonian court records, we had other contemporary writings from those kingdoms as well as records and writings from many of the smaller kingdoms of the region. Unfortunately, when we come to the Persian period, we actually find comparatively few contemporary records. For the earlier period, we also had a large amount of evidence from the Bible. All we have in our biblical records for the Persian era are the books of Ezra/Nehemiah and Esther, along with *possibly* a few references scattered in other books. Little is known about what was going on in the world of the Persian period. Most historical conclusions about this era are tentative.[2]

The chronological order of the ministries of Ezra and Nehemiah present major historical difficulties. An initial reading of the text makes it appear that Ezra returned to Jerusalem first, in the "seventh year of Artaxerxes," while Nehemiah followed later in the "twentieth year of King Artaxerxes" (Ezra 7:7–8; Neh. 2:1). Nehemiah went back to Persia following the completion of his first mission, but came again to Jerusalem in the "thirty-second year of Artaxerxes" (Neh. 13:6–7).

Before considering the evidence related to this issue, we need a table of Persian rulers. Although we do not have much of the details of their reigns, we can be relatively confident of the basic dates of these reigns.

---

1. A detailed study of these two issues is found in William Sandford LaSor, David Allan Hubbard, and Frederick William Bush, *Old Testament Survey* (Eerdmans Publishing Company, 1982), 644–52; compare M. Breneman, *Ezra, Nehemiah, Esther,* The *New American Commentary* 10 (Nashville: Broadman and Holman Publishers, 1993), 42-50.

2. See Edwin M. Yamauchi, *Persia and the Bible* (Grand Rapids: Baker, 1990); Breneman, *Ezra, Nehemiah, Esther,* 15-32.

Persian Chronology	
Cyrus' edict	539
Cambyses	530–522
Darius I	522–486
Ahasuerus (Xerxes)	486–464
Artaxerxes I (Longimanus)	464–423
Darius II	423–404
Artaxerxes II (Mnemon)	404–359
Artaxerxes III	359–

Historians who favor a late date for Ezra point to the following items.

1. On Ezra's return, he found the walls of Jerusalem already rebuilt, but Nehemiah is said to have built the walls (Ezra 9:9; Neh. 6:15).

2. Jerusalem appears to have been deserted in Nehemiah's time but well-populated in that of Ezra (Ezra 10:1; Neh. 7:4).

3. Eliashib was high priest in the time of Nehemiah, while Johanan, the high priest in Ezra's time, is identified as Eliashib's grandson (Ezra 10:6; Neh. 3:1; 12:10–11,22; note that the Hebrew word *ben* son, often means grandson.)

4. Nehemiah's name precedes that of Ezra in Nehemiah 12:26, as if he came first.

5. Nehemiah appointed a commission of treasurers, yet when Ezra arrived in Jerusalem he found such a commission in place (Ezra 8:33; Neh. 13:13).

The evidence is not all one-sided, however. Nehemiah 8 records Ezra's reading of the Law in the time of Nehemiah as if the two were contemporaries.

Three kings of Persia bore the name of Artaxerxes. All interpreters of these books have agreed that Artaxerxes III ruled too late to be considered the king under whom either of these men served. The missions of the two Hebrew leaders simply have to be earlier than his reign. What little we know of the early reign of Artaxerxes III does not at all appear to fit with the conditions in Jerusalem at the time Ezra arrived there.

Many commentators have suggested that Nehemiah returned to Jerusalem in the reign of Artaxerxes I and Ezra came in the time of Artaxerxes II. While this did not solve all the problems, it did appear to solve most of them. This dating of the ministries of the two men, however, has still left us with the conclusion that the initial reading of the text appears that Ezra came first. Much of the evidence that seemed to indicate that Nehemiah preceded Ezra might be explained away. The one that seemed to be insurmountable was the relationship between the High-Priests under which these two served.

A recently discovered list of high priests in Jerusalem from the era we are considering sheds additional light on this issue. Here we find a Johanan who was high priest *before* the Eliashib in Nehemiah's time. This Johanan's father was named Eliashib. Obviously, Johanan and Eliashib were common family names. Now it is clear that Ezra could have returned during the high priesthood of a Johanan who was not Eliashib's grandson.

We can now conclude that Ezra and Nehemiah probably came to Jerusalem in the reign of Artaxerxes I. Ezra most likely returned to Jerusalem in 457 B.C., and Nehemiah's two returns would have been in 444 and 432 B.C. This means that they would have ministered in Jerusalem at the same time, with Ezra being primarily concerned with religious matters and Nehemiah primarily concerned with civil matters. This could explain why their ministries left them basically uninvolved with one another.

Now we are ready to consider the contents of Ezra/Nehemiah as set forth in the following outline.

Content Outline

I. The return under Zerubbabel and the rebuilding of the temple (Ezra 1:1—6:22)
    A. The edict of Cyrus (1:1–4)
    B. Those who returned to Jerusalem (1:5—2:67)
    C. The altar rebuilt and sacrifice restored (2:68—3:13)
    D. Opposition to the rebuilding of the temple (4:1–24)
    E. Prophetic leadership in rebuilding the temple (5:1—6:15)

    F. Temple dedication and Passover celebration (6:16–22)

  II. The return under Ezra and the problem of intermarriage (Ezra 7:1—10:44)

    A. Ezra's return and authority (7:1—8:36)

    B. The problem with intermarriage (9:1—10:44)

 III. Nehemiah's return and the rebuilding of the wall (Neh. 1:1—6:19)

    A. Conditions in Jerusalem (1:1–3)

    B. Nehemiah's distress (1:4—2:8)

    C. Nehemiah's return and survey (2:9–16)

    D. The walls rebuilt in the face of opposition (2:17—6:19)

 IV. Renewal and rededication of the people of Israel (Neh. 7:1—13:3)

    A. Organization and census (7:1–73a)

    B. Rededication of the people led by Ezra (7:73b—10:39)

    C. Organization in Jerusalem (11:1—13:3)

  V. Nehemiah's second return and additional reforms (Neh. 13:4–31)

Summary of Contents

The material of Ezra/Nehemiah does not present one ongoing narrative. Rather, a series of literary/historical pictures reveals a little of what went on at various times during the Persian period. Each picture focuses on the involvement of Jews. Large gaps in time exist between each piece of action. No matter how much the historian might long for additional information, we do not have it. On the other hand, what we have proclaims God's care for His people in times when they were often desperate and faced a most uncertain future.

I. The Return Under Zerubbabel and Rebuilding the Temple (Ezra 1:1—6:22)

The book opens, not in the time of Ezra but much earlier at the end of the Babylonian captivity. Seven features need our consideration due to their effect on that return.

The first is the nature of the captivity. Contrary to what we might expect, the Hebrews in exile in Babylon possessed a great deal of freedom and generally prospered. Allowed to live in their own communities and follow their own ways of life, both culturally and religiously, they generally did whatever they pleased with one exception. They were not allowed to return home. Most of them were so prosperous in Babylon that, when they were allowed to go home, they chose not to do so. Those who did not go gave large sums of money to help their compatriots rebuild the temple and the Jewish homeland (Ezra 1:6).

The second major feature of the initial return was the edict of Cyrus (1:1–4). When Cyrus captured Babylon in 539 B.C., he reversed two Babylonian policies in an effort to consolidate his hold on the newly-captured empire. Babylonians had brought captives to their land from all of their conquered territories. They had also, as a testimony to the "victory" of their god over the gods of the conquered peoples, carried away treasures from the temples of those peoples and destroyed their temples.

After his victory over Babylon, Cyrus established a policy of allowing captives to return to their homelands. This removed large groups of disaffected peoples from the center of his empire and won him the friendship and loyalty of those allowed to go home. Cyrus ordered the temples of the conquered nations to be rebuilt and such of their ancient treasures as could be located to be restored. He intended this not only to win the favor of the captive peoples but to win empowerment from their gods. Jews who returned to Jerusalem to rebuild their nation and their temple were not the only people to profit from Cyrus' edict. Their return fits in with the early policies of the newly established Medo-Persian empire.

The people who returned to Jerusalem following Cyrus' decree present us with the third feature we must consider (1:5—2:67). Sheshbazzar and Zerubbabel were two leaders who participated in the first return. Sheshbazzar, governor appointed by Cyrus (1:8; 2:2; 3:2,8), led the return but was apparently soon replaced by Zerubbabel.[3] The list of those returning with him fea-

---

3. Scholars have long discussed the identity of Zerubbabel and Sheshbazzar as the two names for the same person, but recent scholarship points to two separate leaders. See Tamara Eshkienazi, "Sheshbazzar," the *Anchor Bible Dictionary* 5, 1207-9; S. Japhet, "Sheshbazzar and Zerubbabel—Against the Background of the Historical and Religious Tendencies of Ezra-Nehemiah," *Zeitschrift für die alttestamentliche Wissenschaft* 94 (1992), 66-98; D. M. Howard, Jr., *An Introduction to the Old Testament Historical Books* (1993), 302-4.

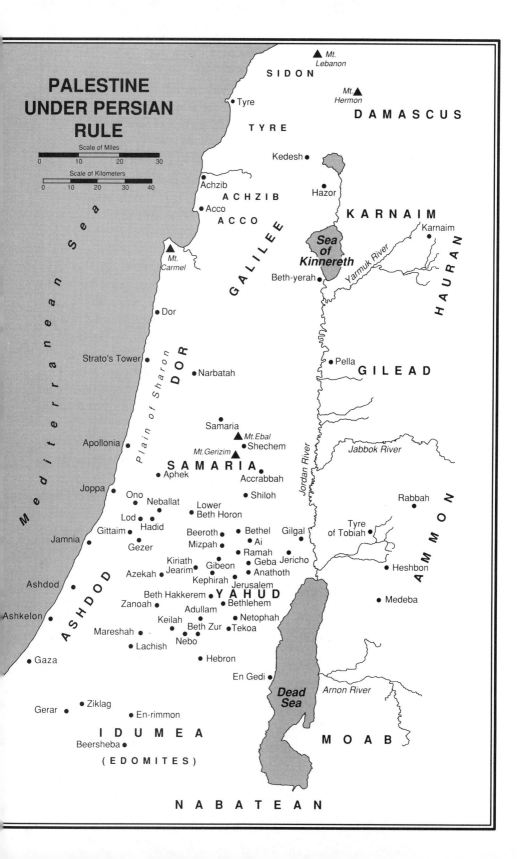

PALESTINE UNDER PERSIAN RULE

Scale of Miles
0   10   20   30

Scale of Kilometers
0   10   20   30   40

Mediterranean Sea

▲ Mt. Lebanon

SIDON

• Tyre

Mt. ▲ Hermon

DAMASCUS

TYRE

Kedesh •

• Hazor

ACHZIB

Achzib •

KARNAIM

• Acco

ACCO

GALILEE

Karnaim •

Sea of Kinnereth

HAURAN

▲ Mt. Carmel

Beth-yerah •

Yarmuk River

• Dor

DOR

Strato's Tower •

Pella •

GILEAD

• Narbatah

Plain of Sharon

Jabbok River

Samaria •
▲ Mt. Ebal
Mt. Gerizim ▲ • Shechem

Apollonia •

SAMARIA

Jordan River

• Aphek
• Accrabbah

Joppa •

• Shiloh

Rabbah •

Ono •
Neballat •

Lower Beth Horon •

Tyre of Tobiah •

AMMON

Lod •
Hadid •

Beeroth •
• Bethel   Gilgal •

Gittaim •

• Ai

Gezer •

Mizpah •
• Ramah

Jericho •

Jamnia •

Kiriath Jearim •
Gibeon •
• Geba
• Anathoth

Heshbon •

Azekah •
Kephirah •
Jerusalem •

Ashdod •

Beth Hakkerem •
YAHUD

ASHDOD

Zanoah •
• Bethlehem

Medeba •

Ashkelon •

Adullam •

Keilah •
Beth Zur • Netophah •
• Tekoa

Mareshah •
Nebo •

• Lachish

• Hebron

Dead Sea

• Gaza

En Gedi •

Arnon River

Gerar •
• Ziklag

• En-rimmon

IDUMEA

Beersheba •

MOAB

(EDOMITES)

NABATEAN

tures priests and Levites, an emphasis already seen in Chronicles and expected in Ezra/Nehemiah. More space is given Levites than to any other family, clan, or tribe among the returnees.

Following the return, the Jews immediately set out to rebuild the altar and restore the regular sacrifices (2:68—3:13) Since their faith made the Hebrews distinctive, the rituals of their faith were the first things they sought to restore. They did not have to use the temple for their rituals.   As soon as the worship system had been restored, Zerubbabel, the political leader, and Jeshua, the priest, led in the rebuilding of the temple (3:8).

Unfortunately, the beginning of the rebuilding of the temple presented the fifth significant feature of the return (4:1–24). This began with the offer from some of the people, probably Samaritans, to join them in the task (4:1–2). Due to the peoples' previous unfaithfulness to God, the returnees rejected their offer. This rejection aroused the Samaritans to initiate a campaign to stop the Jews from rebuilding. The Samaritans tried to convince the Persians that Jewish building would not stop until the city had been fortified against the Persians. The extended opposition ended the rebuilding of the temple for several years.

The Jews accepted the cessation of building more easily because they had already discovered they could carry out their ritual without the temple. Further, Haggai points out that the people had turned from this primary task to that of building their own homes (Hag. 1:1–4).

The sixth feature was the need for the prophetic leadership of Haggai and Zechariah to call the leaders and the people back to the task of rebuilding the temple (5:1—6:15). Apparently, the political and priestly leadership agreed with the policy of suspending the reconstruction of the temple. Prophets rose to lead in renewing the building project. Once again their Samaritan opponents sought to stop the work. This time they were unsuccessful, for King Darius found the original order from Cyrus not only allowing the work but actually ordering it. Darius also ordered his officials to assist with its cost. The rebuilding inspired by the two prophets began in 520 B.C. and was completed in 516 B.C.

The final feature of the narrative of this early return is the actual dedication of the temple, accompanied by the celebration of Passover (6:16–22). Exuberant extravagances marked these two events. In their joy at completing the task they ignored other pressing problems and entered whole-heartedly into celebrating

God's faithfulness and mercy. The dedication, coupled with the Passover, turned their minds to His past blessings as well as to those of the present.

II. The Return Under Ezra and the Problem of Intermarriage (Ezra 7:10–44)

The second literary/historical picture begins almost sixty years after the first, if our earlier dating of Ezra's coming to Jerusalem is correct. These years had passed in the interim between the final verse of chapter 6 and the first verse of chapter 7. (If our dating is wrong, more than sixty years had elapsed.) Again we see inspired writers more concerned with what God was doing than with every event that happened. Modern historians and Bible students would like to know, of course, what happened in those intervening years. The biblical writer was concerned with proclaiming a message, not with recording history in all its details.

Ezra led a new return of Jews from Babylon. These were descendants of those who had not returned with Zerubbabel and Sheshbazzar (7:1—8:36). Ezra is introduced by his genealogy as well as by his profession, being "a scribe skilled in the law of Moses" (7:6). Scribes in Israel were originally court officials, keeping governmental records. By the time of Ezra the term in the Old Testament generally referred to persons who were skilled in copying and interpreting the Torah. Such was Ezra. Given authority by King Artaxerxes to lead a group of returnees and to offer sacrifices in Jerusalem, he carried out his journey as a spiritual ministry.

On his arrival in Jerusalem, Ezra recognized a problem. The Jews in Jerusalem had not kept themselves separate from the people of the land as they had been commanded to do (9:1—10:44; Lev. 20:26). Intermarriage between people of God and pagans had become acceptable as norms. Implication of the text is that having been lax in observing this part of the Law, they were lax in observing all of it.

Ezra immediately expressed his grief at the conditions. He began to deal as quickly and as effectively as possible with what he saw as a spiritual crisis. His solution appears harsh by contemporary standards. The permissive attitude of our society, however, is not the standard expected to be characteristic of Hebrew society. Ezra called a great assembly and demanded that all such illicit marriages be dissolved. While a desperate solution, we must remember that Ezra had not created the situation. Such a solution called vivid attention to the importance of keeping all of God's Law.

III. Nehemiah's Return and the Rebuilding of the Wall (Neh. 1:1—6:19)

The third literary/historical picture of the Ezra/Nehemiah complex introduces Nehemiah, a cup bearer in the service of King Artaxerxes (2:1). Such a servant was highly trusted, having the duty not only of serving the king his wine but of tasting it first to make sure not only that it was good but, more importantly, that it was not poisoned.

Nehemiah was obviously descended from some of the Jews who had earlier remained in Babylon. During his service at the palace in Shushan, he came in contact with some Jewish business-men. Nehemiah discovered that Jerusalem, the beloved holy city of all Jews, was still defenseless (1:3). Some interpreters see this sit-uation as the consequence of some new crisis that had befallen the city. That Hebrew text, however, allows the interpretation that what distressed Nehemiah was merely the ongoing condition of the city, not a new crisis. Ultimately, what distressed Nehemiah was the city was still defenseless almost a century after the initial re-turn.

Nehemiah first expressed his agony to God and then shared it with the king (1:4—2:8). He finally requested and was granted permission to go to Jerusalem to rebuild the city's defenses. This indicates something of the trust that the king had placed in Ne-hemiah.

The journey of Nehemiah, unlike that of Ezra, was apparent-ly without any contingent of Jews who wished to return with him. Nehemiah's journey would most likely have been quite rapid since he was about the king's business as well as his own desires. He ar-rived in Jerusalem in 444 B.C. (2:9–16). Rather than risk arousing opposition too soon, he surveyed the conditions under cover of darkness. We can safely assume that with the letters from the king, he used his authority during the daytime to get verbal reports of those same conditions. He obviously did not wish to begin his mis-sion until he knew exactly what needed to be done.

Having completed his survey of the conditions in Jerusalem, Nehemiah assembled the leaders of the city and told them what he had come for. He organized them and set about the rebuilding of the walls around Jerusalem (2:17—6:19). When Sanballat, the Persian provincial governor of Samaria, and other enemies of the Jews in neighboring regions became aware of the work of rebuilding, they first ridiculed the Jews and then became angry at the progress they were making. In fact, these enemies sought to make a surprise attack on the Jews to stop their work. Nehemiah, however, discovered this. He organized the people not only to rebuild but to defend those who did the rebuilding.

When their military intervention was thwarted, the enemies of the Jews sought to lure Nehemiah away from Jerusalem, possibly intending to assassinate or imprison him. Nehemiah, however, refused to leave his work. Then they tried to undermine his work by accusing the Jews of a treasonous attempt to rebel against Persia. Nehemiah persevered in his task, and the wall around the city was finally completed.

IV. Renewal and Rededication of the People of Israel (Neh. 7:1—13:3)

With the completion of the wall around Jerusalem, the narrative shifts its emphasis with a fourth literary/historical picture. Nehemiah organized the people for defense and service. This involved a census of the people of Jerusalem and its environs (7:1–73). The reason for this census is unknown. Nehemiah probably wanted to assign responsibility for furnishing the supplies needed for the operation of the temple and the city. The Perisan king may have ordered it as part of Nehemiah's official responsibilities. Nehemiah's census list is almost identical with that of the people who returned with Ezra (2:1–70).

At this point, with the physical defense of the city now established, the leaders of Jerusalem turned their attention to its spiritual condition (7:3—10:39). Ezra was asked to bring the Torah and read it to all the people. Following Ezra's reading of the Torah, the people reinstituted the celebration of the Feast of Booths. This, in turn, led to a time of national confession, rededication, and a reaffirmation of their covenant commitment to Yahweh. Nehemiah and Ezra seemed to have been associated here for the first time in a common activity (8:9).

Nehemiah was aware that a larger population was needed for the successful defense of Jerusalem. Thus he and the leaders of the city tried to increase the population of the city, getting it even more organized for both ministry and defense (11:1—13:3). They set up the temple ministry, made sure Jerusalem was defended, and prepared to defend the whole region of Judah. Sometime during this period, Nehemiah apparently decided he had fulfilled the king's commission, so he returned to Shushan (see 13:6).

V. Nehemiah's Second Return and Additional Reforms (Neh. 13:4–31)

Following Nehemiah's return to the service of King Artaxerxes, he heard disturbing news from Jerusalem. Again, he requested permission to go to Jerusalem. His actions on returning lead us to assume that he heard of the Hebrews' laxity in observing their new covenant commitment.

Following his purification of the temple abuses, Nehemiah restored the practice of tithing for the support of the Levites and forced a renewed Sabbath observance. His stringency at this point probably related to the fact that Sabbath observance was considered to be almost as distinctive a characteristic of the Jews as was circumcision. Finally, he sought to enforce the earlier regulations of Ezra regarding foreign marriages. The final summary of this part of his ministry emphasizes that purification of his people was his ultimate purpose on this visit.

Message

Many interpreters see the Books of Ezra and Nehemiah as having little significant and nothing original to proclaim. Such superficial judgment comes from not spending time with these books or not stopping and thinking about what these books actually say. Not as challenging as the stinging words of the prophets or as comforting and uplifting as the Psalms, the Books of Ezra and Nehemiah have a message for those who will listen.

1. As with the other history books of the Old Testament, Ezra and Nehemiah proclaim the absolute sovereignty of God. He is sovereign over those who are His followers as well as over those who have never heard of Him or who have rejected Him.

2. God uses people as His servants regardless of their background or training. This means that a civil servant or a priest can and does have a place in the fulfillment of His plans.

3. God uses different people in different ways in the same general place and time. Such people may be called on to

work independently of one another at some times and at
other times to work together. No one can say that any one
person's work is more important than that of the other.
This is true whether the service rendered at the moment
is physical or spiritual. God is concerned with all of life,
and His servants must be also.

4. Repentance and recommitment are important for the
   people of God. Such spiritual acts lose their value, however, when people do not follow through on decisions
   with a changed life-style. God's servants need to be concerned that God's people fulfill their commitments, leaving their sin behind.

5. God's servants are responsible to God for doing things
   that match their talents, skills, and training. We are responsible for using the gifts God has given.

6. The ultimate basis for fulfilling God's purposes is His
   Word. God's people need to hear God's Word and are expected to act on it.

Ezra and Nehemiah as Individuals

Ezra

In the scattered biblical references, Ezra appears as an aus-
tere scholar dedicated to the copying and study of God's Word,
the Torah. He was a priest, belonging to a family who had remained in Babylon at the time of the first return of the Jews from
Babylonian captivity.   Ezra had used his time in Babylon to become an expert in God's Law.

Learning of the moral and spiritual laxity of the Jews in Jerusalem, Ezra asked for and was granted permission to lead a group
back to his homeland. In addition, he asked for money and authority to carry out his task of reformation. While the Persians
were predisposed to aid former Babylonian exiles, it still would
have required a high degree of courage for Ezra to approach the
king with his requests.

Ezra showed his courage when he faced the dangers of the
long journey home without the protection of an armed guard.
Perhaps his greatest demonstration of courage came when he
faced the people of Jerusalem and demanded that they divorce
their foreign wives. Some suggest that Ezra was a heartless man in

making such demands on his people. Admittedly, he shows no compassion in making those demands. At the same time he had not created the situation. The spiritual laxity of his people required drastic measures to counteract it. While we should refrain from sitting in judgment on the demands of Ezra, we must be aware that he was totally devoted to the Torah with its demands on life. For Ezra, life under God was all black and white, with no shades of gray in between. We need to recognize the absolute need in any society for people who are utterly committed to the study of and obedience to the Word of God.

Nehemiah

Nehemiah is sometimes contrasted with Ezra as being more human and compassionate. This is an unfair and probably an incorrect comparison. Evidence simply does not justify such a conclusion, although other comparisons between the two can justifiably be made. In contrast to Ezra's priestly lineage, Nehemiah was a civil servant in a position of high trust. That he, a Jew, was in such a position in a Persian royal court makes this all the more surprising and points up the outstanding trustworthiness that he must have exemplified.

Nehemiah felt the problems of his people. He took his deepest concerns to God in prayer. While many religious people might stop with feeling and praying, Nehemiah sought to do what he could to deal with the critical needs as he perceived them. He approached his problem carefully and thoughtfully, planning out each step in the process.

In addition, Nehemiah kept his attention on the main task. He neither allowed opposition nor threats to turn him aside. At the same time, he took such opposition seriously and dealt with it as it came. When he had accomplished what he started to do, he was willing to leave other tasks to those better suited to deal with them. He did not perceive power or authority as something to which one should cling.

Finally, Nehemiah is seen as a man with high expectations. He demanded of himself and his people the fulfillment of whatever commitments they had made. He expected the repentant to leave their sin and the committed to stick to their covenants. He carried these expectations into all areas of life: religious, moral, personal, and social.

Questions for Review and Reflection

1. Describe the rise of Cyrus. How did his policies change the history of the Jewish people?

2. Identify the major evidence used to give dates to the ministries of Ezra and Nehemiah. Which dating system do you prefer? What difference does it make to your understanding of the Bible as Scripture if Ezra came later than Nehemiah rather than at the same time?

3. Describe the major accomplishments of Ezra. Of Nehemiah.

4. How does Ezra and Nehemiah's handling of the divorce issue provide teaching for the modern church?

Bibliography

Blenkinsopp, Joseph. *Ezra-Nehemiah: A Commentary. Old Testament Library*. Philadelphia: Westminster, 1988.

Breneman, Mervin. *Ezra. Nehemiah. Esther. New American Commentary*. Nashville: Broadman and Holman Publishers, 1993.

Clines, David J. A. *Ezra, Nehemiah, Esther. New Century Bible Commentary*. Grand Rapids: Eerdmans, 1984.

Fensham, F. Charles. *The Books of Ezra-Nehemiah. New International Commentary*. Grand Rapids: Eerdmans, 1982.

Owens, Mary Frances. *Ezra, Nehemiah, Esther, Job. Layman's Bible Book* Vol. 7) Nashville: Broadman Press, 1983.

Williamson, H. G. M. *Ezra, Nehemiah*. Vol. 16 of *Word Biblical Commentary*. Waco: Word, 1985.

Chapter 9

The Book of Esther

Few, if any, books of the Hebrew Scriptures are as treasured for sheer enjoyment by the Jewish people as is Esther. Jewish people may revere the Torah, sing praises with the Psalms, and find guidance for life in Job and Proverbs; but they give themselves over to Esther in exuberant joy.

Certainly Esther does not deal with such significant historical-theological issues as do Joshua and Judges. Neither does it cover the broad sweep of critical historical periods as do 1 and 2 Samuel, 1 and 2 Kings, or 1 and 2 Chronicles. Yet the exuberant love the Jewish people have for the Book of Esther makes it a subject that deserves serious study. To the Jewish people, it is known simply as "the scroll." No other book of the Old Testament has ever been given this title.

Place in the Canon, Date, and Authorship

Like Ruth, the Book of Esther is located among the Writings, the third section of the Hebrew Scriptures, associated neither with the Deuteronomic complex of Joshua through 2 Kings nor with the Priestly-Levitical complex of 1 Chronicles through Nehemiah. Rather, it is the last of the five little books known in the Hebrew Scriptures as the Megilloth, a term that simply means "The Scrolls." (A brief discussion of the Megilloth is found in chapter

4.)[1] Esther is the only one of the five scrolls of the Megilloth specifically connected with a Jewish festival from the time when it was first written. It appears to have been written to explain how the Feast of Purim originated.

Glossary	
Purium	A joyous festival the Jews celebrated to help them remember their deliverance from Haman's threat to destroy the race.
Ahasuerus	Biblical name for King Xerxes of Persia.
Megilloth	Five scrolls in the Hebrew Bible used to celebrate the Jewish religious festivals. They contain the Books of Ruth, Song of Songs, Ecclesiastes, Lamentations, and Esther.
Maccabean Age	Period when Israel required political independence under the leadership of a family called the Maccabees from 167 to 63 B.C.

The author of the Book of Esther is unknown. An ancient Jewish tradition ascribes it to "the men of the great synagogue," while another suggests that Esther's cousin, Mordecai, wrote it. The book exhibits a careful literary plan, indicating that it probably had only one author. No final conclusion as to his or her identity can be made. The author may have been one of the Jews in Persia descended from the Babylonian exiles. If so, he had survived the anti-Semitic assault that the book is about.

The date of the writing of Esther is almost as difficult to determine as its authorship. The book features the Persian king Xerxes I, the biblical Ahasuerus. Obviously, the book was not written before his reign. Thus, the earliest possible date is 464 B.C., when his reign ended. At the other extreme, Esther appears in the Greek Septuagint sometime after 200 B.C. Neither Esther nor Mordecai were mentioned in the "Hymn to the Fathers" found in Ecclesiasticus. This indicates for some scholars that it had not been written when Ecclesiasticus first appeared about 180 B.C. Ezra,

---

1. A brief introduction to the Megilloth is found in James King West's *Introduction to the Old Testament* (Macmillan Publishing Co., 1981, second ed.), 462–69.

however, was not mentioned in Ecclesiasticus either, and his book was certainly completed before then. Esther was possibly written near the beginning of the period we have identified, with its final editing taking place near the end. Not enough evidence presently exists to allow a conclusion any more precise than this.

Organization

The most surprising issue in the study of Esther is that neither the name Yahweh, nor any other title for God, appears anywhere in the Hebrew text. This is not true of any other book in the Old Testament. Even the very secular Song of Solomon and the cynical Ecclesiastes mention God.

Esther's story is clear that God controls the life and ministry of this beautiful young Hebrew girl and of her cousin Mordecai. Israel's God carefully guided the entire process of thwarting the sadistic plans of the evil Haman to exterminate the Jews. He directed everything to ensure the survival of His people. God's place in the story is so clear to the sensitive reader that it appears the author or editor carefully designed the book so that no word for God appeared.

The omission of God's name or of any word for God led to debate among the rabbis over Esther's place in Scripture. Many of the rabbis felt that a book that did not mention God should not be included. Apparently, Jews accepted Esther as Scripture primarily because it was precious to the ordinary Hebrew. They had heard God speak through its pages and seen Him at work in the deliverance that it recorded.

Some interpreters have suggested that the name and titles for God were left out because the book was written during the Maccabean age. They suggest that in that era the gulf between God and sinful humanity was viewed as being so great that no pious writer would dare to write His name or even to refer to Him. While on the surface that suggestion may sound reasonable, it will not stand close examination. Pious Hebrews wrote many books in that era, and none seem to have been afraid of mentioning God by name or by title.

Perhaps the more likely suggestion for the omission of the name of God in Esther has to do with the use of the book. Esther is read annually at the Jewish Feast of Purim. Purim is without doubt the most exuberant, boisterous feast the Hebrews observed. Some of the celebrants at the feast become quite intoxicated. Perhaps the editor omitted the name of God to avoid any possibility of sacrilege by using God's name under such conditions. While this may not be the correct solution and certainly is not wholly satisfactory as an explanation, it is the best that we have at this time.

Most Christians who read the Book of Esther for the first time are struck by the fierceness of the Jewish revenge on their enemies. This becomes a serious issue for understanding the book and of understanding why it is in the canon. The attitude of the Jews in wreaking such vengeance is a far cry from Jesus' teachings of turning the other cheek (Matt. 5:38–39). Even the Old Testament, while setting forth a concept of justice in the teachings of "an eye for an eye," insists that vengeance is the prerogative of God alone (Ex.. 21:24; Lev. 24:20; Deut. 19:21; 32:35; Ps. 94:1).

In the face of a violent anti-Semitic purge planned by the Persian prime minister, Haman, the Jews were allowed to defend themselves and to strike viciously at their enemies. They responded quickly and with violent enthusiasm. Not only so, the Jews enjoyed it so much that they asked for and were given an additional day to continue the violence (Esth. 9:1–15).

Modern readers can complain: Jesus would not have expected His followers to act like Esther's heroes act. At the same time, anyone who has experienced the atrocities of violent racism can at least understand the desire for vengeance that underlies the entire narrative. Acknowledging the atrocities carried out against the Jews over the centuries, especially in this century, we can also understand why the book is still precious to them. Instead of looking for reasons to complain, we can also look for ways the book can be precious to us.

The most difficult and frustrating issue from the standpoint of a historian is that of the historicity of the story itself. This issue has several facets and has led to a variety of conclusions from interpreters. These vary from seeing Esther's story as pure fiction to seeing it as historical narrative and nothing more.

Several major difficulties in the Book of Esther have created the problem.

1. No queen by the names of either Vashti or Esther are found anywhere in the Persian records.
2. According to Herodotus, Xerxes' queen was the daughter of a general in the Persian army, and her name was Amestris.

3. No record exists of a prime minister or any other counselor in Xerxes' court known either as Haman or Mordecai.

4. No record has been found of a planned or actual anti-Semitic campaign in the reign of Xerxes.

5. No record has been found of a campaign of violence carried out by Jews against their enemies in the kingdom.

6. No reference is made in the biblical text to the most significant military campaign of Xerxes, his unsuccessful invasion of Macedonia. This, according to the dating of the biblical narrative, took place at approximately the same time as the earlier events of the book.

Let us consider what we do know of this period and of the biblical narrative.[2]

Names are not always consistent in ancient narratives, particularly in those that carry over from one language to another. Xerxes is known as Ahasuerus in the Bible. People frequently had more than one name. In addition, the official queen of a nation was not necessarily the chief or favorite wife of a king's harem. Esther and Vashti could have filled this role rather than that of royal queen. At the same time, to one writing such a book, the woman married to a king could legitimately be called a queen.

We have frequently noted in our study of the Old Testament history books that Old Testament historians did not simply write history for the sake of history. They wrote of events in which God was involved with His people and through which He was revealing His will and purpose in some way. The fact that Esther makes no reference to Xerxes' Greek campaigns, while it may concern the historian, should be of no concern to the biblical interpreter.

Arguments from silence are always dangerous. The absence of evidence does not prove anything. Persian records of this era are admittedly sparse. Finally, studies of Herodotus have shown he was not the most accurate historian. He seems to err more often by inventing history than by leaving it out.

On a positive note, two additional items must be considered. Contrary to what some writers have suggested, the author of Es-

---

2. See n. 2 of ch. 8, 117. The question of history versus fiction in Esther is discussed by Mervin Breneman, *Ezra. Nehemiah. Esther,* New American Commentary 10 (1993), 278–88. M. V. Fox, *Character and Ideology in the Book of Esther,* Studies on Personalities of the Old Testament (Columbia: University of South Carolina Press, 1991), 131–39; David Howard, Jr., *An Introduction to the Old Testament Historical Books.* (1993), 318–22.

ther was familiar with policies and internal operations of the Persian royal court and knew the appropriate titles of officials and governmental entities. Further, an important development has come to light, having been set in a recent announcement by Ungnad. He had translated an undated cuneiform text that contained a reference to a high official in the court of Xerxes I by the name of Mordecai.[3] Thus we now may have an external historical reference to one of the main Jewish characters of the Book of Esther. This certainly does not prove the historicity of the book, but it begins to undercut the main problems that have been raised.

The best conclusion at the present appears to be that the author of Esther, like the other Old Testament histories, began with a record of events that had occurred at Susa, the capital of the Persian empire. Rather than writing a history of those events according to modern standards of historiography, he proclaimed a message from God through the medium of history.

Having considered the major issues involved in understanding and interpreting Esther, we are ready to consider the basic structure of the book and its message. The following outline will prove helpful.

    I. Esther becomes queen of Persia (1:1—2:23)

        A. The king's banquet (1:1–9)

        B. Queen Vashti ousted (1:10–22)

        C. Searching for a successor (2:1–4)

        D. Esther and Mordecai (2:5–7)

        E. Esther selected as queen (2:8–18)

        F. Mordecai saves the king (2:19–23)

   II. Haman's plot to exterminate the Jews (3:1—5:14)

        A. Haman's hatred of the Jews (3:1–6)

        B. The royal decree of Jewish extermination (3:7–15)

        C. Esther's decision to intercede (4:1–17)

        D. Esther's plan begun (5:1–8)

        E. Haman gloats in his success (5:9–14)

---

3. William Sandford LaSor, David Allan Hubbard, and Frederic Bush, *Old Testament Survey* (Eerdmans Publishing Company, 1982), p. 626; "Mordecai," *The Interpreter's Dictionary of the Bible* (Abingdon Press, 1962), vol. 3, 437–83; David J. A. Clines, "Mordecai," *The Anchor Bible Dictionary* 4 (1992), 902–4 denies the probability of the equation but gives full and recent information.

III. Mordecai and Esther transform the Jews' plight (6:1—8:17)
   A. The king remembers his obligation (6:1–3)
   B. Haman ordered to honor Mordecai (6:4–14)
   C. Esther's entreaty (7:1–4)
   D. Haman executed (7:5–10)
   E. Mordecai elevated to power (8:1–2)
   F. A proclamation to save the Jews (8:3–14)
   G. Celebration among the Jews (8:15–17)
IV. Jewish vengeance on their enemies (9:1—10:3)
   A. Jewish vengeance on their enemies (9:1–10)
   B. The time for vengeance extended (9:11–16)
   C. The Feast of Purim established (9:17–32)
   D. Mordecai's position of power (10:1–3)

Summary of Contents

The Book of Esther gives a fascinating account of the origin of the Jewish Feast of Purim. The story recounts how an unknown Jewish girl rose to be queen of Persia and utilized that position to deliver her people from a vicious outbreak of anti-Semitism.

I. Esther Becomes Queen of Persia (1:1—2:23)

Due to her disobedience, Vashti was deposed as queen of Persia. Following this, King Ahasuerus instituted a search for a new queen. While all details are not recorded, the search took four years (1:3; 2:16).

Esther appears as a part of this search process. She was an orphan who had been reared by her cousin Mordecai. Her Hebrew name was Hadassah (Myrtle), and her Persian name was Esther (star). Eventually, Esther was selected as Vashti's successor. The author carefully noted that she did not reveal her Jewish heritage to the king or his officers. Almost as an afterthought, we learn that during this time Esther's cousin Mordecai discovered a plot to assassinate the king and revealed it to him, saving his life.

II. Haman's Plot to Exterminate the Jews (3:1—5:14)

Haman, the fourth major character, strides into action. Promoted to prime minister of Persia, his pride was injured when Mordecai refused to bow before him. Discovering that his Jewish faith prompted Mordecai's action, Haman, his hatred aroused, set in motion a plan to exterminate all Jews.

With an argument made up of half-truths and exaggerations, Haman led King Ahasuerus to issue a royal edict ordering the extermination of Jews and the seizure of all of their goods. Learning of the edict, Esther faced a dilemma. Under Persian law, no one, not even the queen, could enter the king's presence uninvited. To do so placed one under the threat of death. Mordecai appealed to her to act for her people. His words are memorable for their confidence in God's providential care:

> For if you keep silence at such a time as this, relief and deliverance will rise for the Jews from another quarter. . . . Who knows? Perhaps you have come to royal dignity for just such a time as this? (4:14)

Esther's answer to her cousin is equally as memorable, expressing the utter submission to God of a willing servant. She made her decision to go to the king, interceding for her people. "I will go to the king, though it is against the law; and if I perish, I perish" (4:16). She did not act precipitously. She prayed, was patient, and carried out a carefully prepared plan of action. In the meantime, Haman, thinking everything was going his way, gloated over his continuing success.

III. Mordecai and Esther Transform the Jews' Plight (6:1—8:17)

At this point, Haman's fortunes began to turn. First, the king during a restless night remembered the obligation he owed Mordecai for the warning that had saved his life. Then, in a strange twist of fate, the king ordered Haman to go honor Mordecai on his behalf (6:10–14).

At this point, Esther brought her plan to fruition. She confronted the king with her plight as a Jew and pointed out Haman as the creator of her problems. In his anger at having been misled, King Ahasuerus had Haman executed and elevated Mordecai to Haman's position in the royal council.

The Jews still faced the coming time of persecution. The laws of the Persians were absolutely unchangeable, and thus the edict ordering their persecution could not be repealed. The king issued orders allowing the Jews to arm themselves and to defend themselves against the forthcoming assault of their enemies. Jews were not allowed to attack, but they were given permission to defend themselves.

IV. Jewish Vengeance on Their Enemies (9:1—10:3)

On the day of persecution, the new edict resulted in the Jews striking back with fulfilling vengeance. Not satisfied with the results of that day, Esther asked for an additional day for Jewish revenge.

When the conflict was over, the Jews celebrated their victory. Because the experience was so memorable they instituted a new celebration in their calendar of religious festivals. Here we see the author's primary purpose in writing this book. He wanted to establish the basis for the Feast of Purim.

The book closes with a summary of Mordecai's ultimate position of power and of his ministry to the kingdom.

Message

The primary message of Esther focuses on the awesome providence of God. People do not have to be aware of God's work for Him to be at work. He can and does take the apparently insurmountable crises that come our way and transforms them into opportunities for significant ministry.

In addition, the book points up the need for servants of God who are willing to offer themselves fully. Both Esther and Mordecai went about their normal affairs with a quiet dedication which allowed them to be used in God's ultimate plans. They were forced to take dangerous stands and did so with no show. We need to be willing to take advantage of every opportunity that comes as one for which God has been preparing us throughout our lives.

Esther as an Individual

Esther stands out as a heroine in a time when society was generally patriarchal and women were not expected to have an opportunity for leadership or public service. Not only did she face what was a handicap at that time, being a woman, she was also orphaned, probably at birth. This meant that she had no legal standing in her own community. She had an older, loving cousin, Mordecai, who nurtured her. What might have been considered her third handicap was the fact that she was a Jew growing up in a foreign land. Not only so, as she was growing up, a rising tide of anti-Semitism grew.

Esther was a beautiful young lady with a personality that attracted attention and won the favor even of those who might have been her enemies. When the king began a search for a new queen, Esther was one of the young ladies selected as candidates. After a four-year search, she was found to be pleasing to the king and was elevated to the most exalted position a woman could attain in the Persian empire.

Faced with the threatened storm of anti-Semitism, Esther was encouraged by her cousin to act. Bravely risking death, she went to the king and sought his favor. Showing herself to be both a devoted servant of God and a careful, thoughtful planner, she eventually informed the king that she was a Jew and that her people were about to be exterminated like vermin because of the king's foolish edict. The end result was that she became the instrument by which her people were delivered from the violent persecution of their enemies. Rising above what might have been considered her handicaps, she became, not the victim of her situation, but the victor over it. In so doing, she has become the heroine of every girl or woman who would like to accomplish those things for God that are normally assumed to be the right and privilege of men only.

Questions for Reflection and Review

1. Give the options for dating the writing of the Book of Esther. What evidence is there to help us determine the date? What difference does determining the date of writing make for the interpreter?

2. Do you think it was significant for the author that the hero of the story was female? Would the story have had the same effect if the hero had been male?

3. What significance do you place on the story not mentioning the name of God? Do you think this was an intentional action by the author? In what way does the fact influence your interpretation of the meaning of the story? How can you justify calling the book part of the Word of God if God does not appear in the story?

4. List the arguments for the historicity and for the fictionality of the narrative of Esther. Which arguments do you consider to carry the most weight? What conclusions do

you draw from the argument? How would your interpretation of the meaning and authority of the narrative change if it could be proved that the story is an intentional work of fiction?

5. The question of anti-Semitism and violent reaction carries the plot of the narrative. Why are these subjects treated in Scripture? Can you justify the inclusion of such violent reaction in Scripture? How or why not? Does such teaching have application for modern life?

6. The ultimate reason for writing the Book of Esther appears to be the justification for celebrating the Feast of Purim, a feast whose celebrations often exceeded recommended limits of human sobriety and whose origins could not be traced to the Pentateuch. How can a book with such a limited purpose provide teaching for modern readers?

Bibliography

Baldwin, Joyce G. *Esther: An Introduction and Commentary.* Downer's Grove: Inter-Varsity Press, 1984.

Breneman, Mervin. *Ezra. Nehemiah. Esther. The New American Commentary.* Nashville: Broadman and Holman Publishers, 1993.

Clines, David J. A. *Ezra, Nehemiah, Esther. New Century Bible Commentary.* Grand Rapids: Eerdmans, 1984.

Owens, Mary Frances. *Ezra, Nehemiah, Esther, Job.* Vol. 7 of *Layman's Bible Book Commentary.* Nashville: Broadman Press, 1983.

Chapter 10

The Message
of the History Books

The end of our introduction to the history books of the Old Testament poses one last question. "Why are these books here in the first place?" To phrase it more from the standpoint of faith, we might ask, "What is God saying to us through these books?" That anyone would ask such questions presupposes a basic belief that God's revelation is too important for Him to waste time recording and preserving something that does not reveal and affirm truth about Him and His purposes for humanity.

Some might consider this presupposition to be too presumptuous. On the other hand, we must remind ourselves that over the centuries, multiple communities of faith have treasured these books because they believed that they heard God speak in them. Over those same centuries, devoted scribes and scholars have given themselves to the preservation, study, understanding, and communication of truths that they have found. These facts alone should lead us to ask the questions we have raised.

Admittedly, these books have not been treasured for the praise and inspiration that the Psalms communicate. Neither have they been searched through for the comfort and peace found in the Gospels. They certainly have not been found to be as challenging and demanding as the stinging words of the prophets. Yet, they have been kept and treasured. Saints of all the ages and from all over the world have claimed to have heard God speak through them.

Old Testament historians recorded history not for itself alone but for what God was doing in and through it. Therefore, with each of the books we have studied, we have sought to affirm and identify the basic message that they were, and are, proclaiming. We come to the time to look at all of them together. They were collected and preserved ultimately in the form and order in which we now find them. As we draw this study to a close, we are seeking to identify the overall message they proclaim.

Six major concepts seem to me to be the basic faith proclamation of the Old Testament history books.

The God Who Is Sovereign. —Without question, the primary proclamation of the Old Testament history books is the sovereignty of God. The entire collection announces that Yahweh, the covenant God of Israel, is sovereign over all nature and all history. His sovereignty over nature is shown with droughts and floods, with assaults by locusts, and with numerous nature miracles. His sovereignty over history becomes apparent as He utilizes foreign kings and peoples as instruments of judgment and blessing.

The history books reveal that God's sovereign acts are not mere whims on His part. Israel's neighbors understood their gods to be capricious and undependable. The God of Israel was simply not like this. He was dependable. His demands and expectations were consistent. An even more significant revelation taught that God's love motivated His sovereign acts of power. The sovereign love of God was seen in His loving choices and in His covenant commitment. Out of His grace, He committed Himself to His people. That was good news indeed.

Ultimately, God revealed His sovereign love and power by giving Israel their land and making them into a kingdom. He freely and lovingly took former slaves and made them into a nation of His own choice. Those who had not been a people were made into the people of God. From the Christian perspective, that was but a foreshadowing of the fact that finally He would take a new people and make them into the new people of God (1 Pet.1:10).

Perhaps the last aspect of Yahweh's sovereignty proclaimed by the historical books of the Old Testament is His providence. By this we mean that God controls and moves people, nations, and natural events for the purpose of fulfilling His purposes. This is true whether we are considering Hebrew leaders such as Deborah, David, Nehemiah, and Esther, alien pagans such as Ruth and Cyrus, or natural events such as earthquakes and locust plagues. While not infringing on human choices or human freedom, God moves the right person at the right place at the right time. That, too, is a part of His sovereignty.

The Sin and Rebellion of Israel and the Nations. —In stark contrast to the proclamation of the Old Testament history books that God is sovereign is their proclamation concerning the plight of humanity in general and of Israel in particular. People are seen as being faithless, undependable, and sinful and rebellious.

Yahweh chose Israel to be His people from among all the peoples of the earth. To seal that choice, they entered into a covenant relation with the God who had chosen them. That covenant was treasured and periodically renewed. Israel, however, over and over again violated their covenant commitment with God. This was disobedience at the very least and was outright treachery and rebellion at the worst. While God's relation to Israel was most commonly seen as one of loving choice, Israel's response to Him is most often characterized by sin.

Israel seems always to have failed to remember that under the covenant and under the sovereignty of God sin brings consequences. Those consequences are most often described in the history books in terms of temporal judgment. The point was that God's covenant offered blessings for obedience and punishment or curses for disobedience. (We shall return to this in more detail later in this chapter.) In any case, the almost constant testimony of the history books was that Israel was in rebellion against God. This was especially disastrous due to their special relation with God.

Furthermore, the historical books regularly reveal that other people are responsible to God as well as Israel. Even though Moab, Edom, Syria, Assyria, Babylon, and Persia were not in a covenant relation with Yahweh, they were still sinful. The proclamation was that all people were in sin. Although Israel's sin may have been worse because of their covenant violation, sin was and is the common human plight. Second only to the affirmation of God's sovereignty is the clarity of the revelation of human sin.

The Servants of God. —Most frequently the History Books emphasize the relationship between Yahweh and His human servants. God raises up servants when He sees a need to be filled, an opportunity to be met, or a service to be rendered. These books make several related but distinctive proclamations concerning God and His servants.

1. Related to the sovereignty of God is the revelation that God chooses His servants. This is always seen as His prerogative. Much as a carpenter chooses particular tools to do specific tasks, so God chooses those whom He wishes to use in service.

2. The servants God chooses are quite diverse. These servants included a military leader like Joshua, a scribe like Ezra, a common person like Esther, a prophetess like Deborah, and a shepherd like David. Each one is an individual bringing his or her own unique nature to the task at hand.

3. God chooses people whom He has gifted in a special way and whose experiences have prepared them for the task at hand. Not only are God's servants unique, their individual experiences have prepared them for the task that God assigned them. God is economical, not wasting either the gifts or the preparation of those who serve Him.

4. These books reveal the freedom God gives to those whom He wishes to serve Him. Ahaz had a chance to lead forth in faith but, rather than surrendering to God's purposes, he sought to work things out for himself. David at one point turned aside from his surrender to God and sinned with Bathsheba. God's servants are expected to surrender to His purposes, but they are free to turn aside in disobedience and rebellion. When they do, they must face the consequences inherent in their choices and actions. (We will return to this idea later.) The History Books want us to know that God expects His servants to be obedient.

5. In raising up His servants, God calls them to leadership for the moment, whatever that moment may be. God's choice is not necessarily for the entire life of His servants. Some are chosen for a brief period of service, while others are asked to give all of their lives.

6. No servant is indispensable for God's kingdom. Leaders may die or become ineffective, but such human frailties do not halt God's work. Joshua's death did not end Isra-

el's occupation of the land. David's sin did not destroy the monarchy, nor did Manasseh's apostasy bring God's work with His people to a halt. Workers may die or fail, but God's work goes on.

7. The history books of the Old Testament clearly call attention to events and what God was doing in them. They often focus, however, on the part His prophets played in those events. In every age and in every situation, God raised up His prophets. The leaders and the people were never without someone to share God's will and purposes and to call them back to Him in repentance.

8. These books also reveal that worship is important for the people of God. Those who lead worship are called to purity and faithfulness like all of God's servants. These books clearly proclaim that worship is no substitute for obedience. We cannot cover up our sin and disobedient rebellion by merely going through the proper forms of worship. Obedience to God's will and commands is the first step in worship. Without obedience, there can be no real worship.

9, The last aspect of God's relation with his servants is that in their service of God they are expected to be models in their human relationships. God uses the human love they have for others to accomplish His purposes. God used Ruth's love for Naomi, Esther's love for her people, and Josiah's love for his nation as a major part of their service.

God's Anger, Judgment, and Deliverance.— One of the features of Old Testament faith that often troubles modern interpreters is its emphasis on judgment. Many modern commentators find it difficult to believe that a God of love would involve Himself with judgment. The Bible student must deal with hard evidence from the text. The historical books are filled with an emphasis on God's wrath and its subsequent effect, His judgment.

The first feature presented in this connection by the Old Testament history books is that Israel's sin, rebellion, and infidelity aroused the anger of God. Unlike human anger, God's anger never gets out of control. It is simply His passionate reaction to human sin. The point clearly made by these books is that God cares deeply about His people and, therefore, cares about their almost habitual disobedience and apostasy. Thus Yahweh's anger is real, but we must never forget that, unlike the gods of the pagans that surrounded Israel, the anger of Yahweh is never irrational. His anger always arises from His covenant love.

The second feature of significance is that God's anger leads to His temporal judgment on His people. Moses' sermon on the plains of Moab clearly warned Israel that their obedience or disobedience to the covenant resulted in God's blessing or curses. They would be blessed by obedience and cursed by disobedience (Deut. 27:15—28:6). Everyone could understand that.

The third feature proclaimed by these books is that faithfulness is important. Israel was expected to be faithful just as God was always faithful. God, being faithful and dependable, kept His promises. He expected His people to keep their covenant promises.

The fourth proclamation of the history books is that His promises made both judgment and hope for deliverance a reality for Israel. Because God was faithful, He would judge and punish an unfaithful people. Similarly, because He was faithful to His covenant, they could believe in His deliverance promised through the prophets. Each time deliverance became reality, whether from the Philistines or from the Babylonian captivity, Israel gained new hope for the future. God would not abandon them, for He ultimately promised good to them. If His promised judgments came to pass, promised deliverance would also. Even in the darkest days of defeat and foreign domination, God's promised deliverance radiated hope on the people of Israel. While hopeful expectation is not an overwhelmingly major feature of the history books, it is present in them and was a part of their proclamation.

God's Future and Humanity's Hope.— Arising out of the historical books' proclamation of Yahweh's dependability and trustworthiness was a message of future hope. These books consistently reveal God as One who brought order out of chaos. This Divine characteristic was revealed in every part of Israel's history: in the chaos of Israel's invasion of Canaan, in the chaos of Philistine, Syrian, Assyrian, and Babylonian conquests, in the chaos of famine and drought, and in the chaos of an anti-Semitic purge. Since Israel had seen God act in these ways, they had reason to hope despite present chaos that many would identify as hopeless.

The Hebrew monarchy's ultimate defeat brought a new dimension to Israel's understanding of God. The nations of the ancient Near East shared a common belief that the defeat of a nation meant that their god had been defeated by the god of the conquerors. Israel learned that this was not so. Their defeat did not mean the defeat of God. The defeat of Israel was an example of God's sovereign power, for He had used the forces of a pagan nation to bring His judgment on His people.

The historical books also revealed that although messages change, God does not. As Israel's historical and spiritual circumstances changed from era to era, the proclamation of the prophets altered. The God behind their messages remained consistent. The changing human situation, not the changing of God, demanded different messages.

The Authoritative Word.—Intimately related to all of the foregoing teachings of the Old Testament historical books and clearly undergirding them is the proclamation of these books that God's Word is authoritative. This may be most clearly visible in the Priestly-Levitical histories with their emphasis on the absolute authority of the Torah. The Deuteronomic history presents exactly the same proclamation in the fact that the curses of Deuteronomy consistently came to pass on unfaithful Israel.

The ultimate authority of God's Word for all of Israel's faith and practice gave rise to the emphasis of this collection on repentance and reform. Because God's Word was authoritative, the people of Israel were consistently called on to repent of their sin and rebellion, following this with national and personal reform. Such reforms were consistently seen as being ultimately ineffective. The need for them gave rise to the realization that in some way God was going to intervene to transform His people.

Perhaps the ultimate message of these books can be summed up in the following words that they proclaim. Has the Lord as great delight in burnt offerings and sacrifices, as in obeying the voice of the Lord?

> Surely, to obey is better than sacrifice,
> and to heed than the fat of rams.
> (1 Sam. 15:22)

> And the Lord came and stood forth, calling . . .
> And Samuel said,
> "Speak, for thy servant is listening" (1 Sam 3:10).

> My heart exults in the Lord;
> my strength is exalted in my God.
> My mouth derides my enemies,
> because I rejoice in my victory.
> (1 Sam. 2:1)

Isaiah's words may have summed all of these proclamations up best.

> The grass withers, the flower fades;
> but the word of our God will
> stand for ever.
> (Isa. 40:8)

Questions for Reflection and Review

1. Choose one of Cate's conclusions above. Find at least five examples in the historical books that support the conclusion. Can you find examples that question or qualify the conclusion?

2. Which of Cate's conclusions has the most meaning for your life of faith and doubt? Use examples from your own life history to show the truth of the biblical teaching. What examples from your life would you use to call the conclusion into question? How would you try to reconcile the difference from your experience and this teaching?

3. Define the task of a writer of the history of the conflict in Viet Nam. How does that job assignment differ from the assignment of the writers of biblical history? Define the task of the biblical historian. What does that say about the sources used and the fidelity in reporting historical events?

4. Choose a narrative from 1 or 2 Kings that has a parallel in 1 or 2 Chronicles. Describe the similarities and distinctions in the two accounts. Explain why you think such distinctions exist. How does recognizing the differences help you understand the purpose of each biblical writer?

5. Write a note to a close friend or family member summarizing the most important points you have learned from the study of the historical books of the Old Testament. Why is each point important to you?

Bibliography

General Works

Anderson, G. W., ed. *Tradition and Interpretation.* Oxford: Clarendon Press, 1979.

Baly, Dennis. *God and History in the Old Testament.* San Francisco: Harper and Row, Publishers, 1976.

Cate, Robert L. *Old Testament Roots for New Testament Faith.* Nashville: Broadman Press, 1982.

_____. *How to Interpret the Bible.* Nashville: Broadman Press, 1983.

Crockett, William Day. *A Harmony of Samuel, Kings, and Chronicles.* Grand Rapids: Baker Book House, 1975.

Wiseman, D. J., ed. *Peoples of Old Testament Times.* London: Oxford University Press, 1975.

Archaeology and Geography

Baly, Dennis. *The Geography of the Bible.* New York: Harper and Brothers Publishers, 1957.

Cornfeld, Gaalyah. *Archaeology of the Bible: Book by Book.* San Francisco: Harper and Row Publishers, 1976.

Finkelstein, Israel. *The Archaeology of the Israelite Settlement.* Jerusalem: Israelite Exploration Society, 1988.

Frank, Harry Thomas. *Atlas of the Bible Lands.* Nashville: Broadman Press, 1977.

May, Herbert G. *Oxford Bible Atlas*. London: Oxford University Press, 1976.

Mazar, Amihai. *Archaeology of the Land of the Bible 10,000–586 B.C.* New York: Doubleday, 1990.

Wright, G. Ernest and Floyd V. Filson, eds. *Westminster Historical Maps of Bible Lands*. Philadelphia: The Westminster Press, 1952.

Old Testament History

Bright, John. *A History of Israel*. 3rd ed. Philadelphia: The Westminster Press, 1981.

Bruce, F. F. *Israel and the Nations*. Grand Rapids: William B. Eerdmans Publishing Company, 1963.

Cate, Robert L. *These Sought a Country: A History of Israel in Old Testament Times*. Nashville: Broadman Press, 1985.

Dearman, J. Andrew. *Religion and Culture in Ancient Israel*. Peabody, Mass.: Hendrickson, 1992).

Gordon, Cyrus H. *Introduction to Old Testament Times*. Ventnor: Ventnor Publishers, Inc., 1953.

Hayes, John H. and J. Maxwell Miller. *Israelite and Judean History*. Philadelphia: The Westminster Press, 1977.

_____, and Paul K. Hooker. *A New Chronology for the Kings of Israel and Judah*. Atlanta: John Knox Press, 1988.

Heaton, E. W. *The Hebrew Kingdoms*. London: Oxford University Press, 1968.

Hermann, Siegfried. *The History of Israel in Old Testament Times*. Translated by John Bowden. Philadelphia: Fortress Press, 1975.

_____. *Time and History*. Trans. James L. Blevins. Nashville: Abingdon, 1981.

Jaegersma, Henk. *A History of Israel in the Old Testament Period*. Translated by John Bowden. Philadelphia: Fortress Press, 1983.

Soggin, J. A. *A History of Ancient Israel*. Trans. John Bowden. Philadelphia: Westminster Press, 1984.

Thiele, Edwin R. *The Mysterious Numbers of the Hebrew Kings*. Rev. ed. Grand Rapids: Zondervan, 1983.

Old Testament Introduction

Anderson, Bernhard W. *Understanding the Old Testament*. 4th ed. Englewood Cliffs: Prentice-Hall, 1986.

Archer, Gleason L., Jr. *A Survey of Old Testament Introduction*. Chicago: Moody Press, 1964.

Brueggemann, Walter, and Hans Walter Wolff. *The Vitality of Old Testament Traditions*. Atlanta: John Knox Press, 1975.

Cate, Robert L. *An Introduction to the Old Testament and Its Study*. Nashville: Broadman Press, 1987.

Childs, Brevard S. *Introduction to the Old Testament as Scripture*. Philadelphia: Fortress Press, 1979.

Crenshaw, James L. *Story and Faith*. New York: Macmillan Publishing Co., Inc., 1986.

Flanders, Henry Jackson, Jr., Robert Wilson Crapps, and David Anthony Smith. *People of the Covenant*. 3rd ed. Oxford: Oxford University Press, 1988.

Francisco, Clyde T. *Introducing the Old Testament*. Rev. ed. Nashville: Broadman Press, 1977.

Gottwald, Norman K. *The Hebrew Bible: A Socio-Literary Introduction*. Philadelphia: Fortress Press, 1985.

Harrelson, Walter. *Interpreting the Old Testament*. New York: Holt, Rinehart and Winston, Inc., 1964.

Hill, Andrew E. and Walton, John H. *A Survey of the Old Testament*. Grand Rapids: Zondervan, 1991.

House, Paul. *Old Testament Survey*. Nashville: Broadman Press, 1991.

Humphreys, W. Lee. *Crisis and Story*. Palo Alto: Mayfield Publishing Company, 1979.

La Sor, William Sanford, David Allan Hubbard, and Frederic William Bush. *Old Testament Survey*. Grand Rapids: William B. Eerdmans Publishing Co., 1982.

Napier, Davie. *Song of the Vineyard: A Guide through the Old Testament*. Rev. ed. Philadelphia: Fortress Press, 1981.

Rogerson, John, ed. *Beginning Old Testament Study*. Philadelphia: The Westminster Press, 1982.

West, James King. *Introduction to the Old Testament*. 2nd ed. New York: Macmillan Publishing Co., Inc., 1981.

Young, Edward J. *An Introduction to the Old Testament*. Rev. ed. Grand Rapids: William B. Eerdmans Publishing Co., 1964.

Scripture Index

Ruth

1 Samuel

2 Samuel